# Slow

# Gennaro Contaldo

# Slow

EASY, COMFORTING ITALIAN MEALS WORTH WAITING FOR

PAVILION

# CONTENTS

# CONVERTING COOKING TIMES

## PRESSURE COOKER
HIGH PRESSURE ( 15PSI )

## OVEN
160°C FAN / 180°C  -  GAS MARK 4 ( 350°F )

## OVEN
140°C FAN / 160°C  -  GAS MARK 3 ( 325°F )

## SLOW COOKER
HIGH 90°C / 194°F

## SLOW COOKER
MEDIUM 84°C / 183°F

## SLOW COOKER
LOW 77°C / 171°F

| 10 MINS | 20 MINS | 30 MINS | 40 MINS | 50 MINS | 1 HOUR |
|---------|---------|---------|---------|---------|--------|
| 30 MINS | 1 HOUR | 1½ HOURS | 2 HOURS | 2½ HOURS | 3 HOURS |
| 35 MINS | 1 HOUR & 10 MINS | 1 HOUR & 45 MINS | 2 HOURS & 20 MINS | 2 HOURS & 55 MINS | 3½ HOURS |
| 2 HOURS | 2½ HOURS | 3 HOURS | 3½ HOURS | 4 HOURS | 4½ HOURS |
| 3 HOURS | 4 HOURS | 4½ HOURS | 5 HOURS | 6 HOURS | 7 HOURS |
| 4 HOURS | 5 HOURS | 6 HOURS | 7 HOURS | 8 HOURS | 9 HOURS |

# Introduction

Slow cooking is one of my favourite ways to cook: it's simple, stress-free and allows you to get on with other things safe in the knowledge that slowly, slowly the stove-top or oven is doing its job. Stews and sauces bubble on the hob, a roast cooks in the oven with herbs gently infusing the meat, breads and cakes bake, all filling the house with mouth-watering smells and creating that special warmth which nothing else can.

It takes me back in time to when – only a generation or so ago – everyone cooked on coals and wood. There was no gas or electricity, and food sometimes took all day (or even all night) to cook. Soups gently simmered on wood-burning stoves, potatoes were baked in the ash from the day's fire, and whole animals were cooked in underground pits.

My mother, grandmother, aunt and sisters would leave a ragù or soup very gently bubbling on the hob so that there was always a hot meal ready, whatever time the rest of the family got home. Delicious cooking smells filled the house, giving it that warm and cosy feeling of home and all that is good and wholesome; a bad day at school or work would somehow be soothed away.

When I was in my teens, people in the village, including my family, were changing their kitchens and the latest trend was to have a new gas cooker incorporating stove-top and oven in the same unit. Huge green gas cylinders were hauled up the stairs of apartments and attached to the cooker. There was much excitement as people talked about their new 'American' gadget that made cooking much quicker. The flame was instant and it was no longer necessary to light a fire.

Gradually, over the years, supplies of coal and wood were replaced with the cylinders. Shrewd housewives always kept a spare, especially during winter and feast times. My grandfather refused to change, and kept the same old range; this is where the family got together for Sunday lunches and special occasions until he died in the early 1980s. At the time, I could not believe he would forgo such luxury. It was not until years later, as an adult and chef, that I looked back with much fondness and nostalgia at that old kitchen range – the romance of the flickering flame, the warmth of a real fire, the smell of burning wood and ash. That's why, a few years ago, I had a rustic kitchen built in my garden with a wood-fired oven and stove; now I can recreate those slow, slow-cooked dishes of my childhood using copper pans and terracotta pots, and enjoy the oh-so-wonderful smells of freshly baked bread from the wood oven.

## Pulses – soaking and simmering

Dried beans, chickpeas and lentils, soaked overnight in preparation for the next day's meal, are an essential and economical part of the slow-cooking repertoire. Pulses were especially important during the winter, when fresh vegetables were in shorter supply, and to ensure a varied diet we always kept a selection in our store cupboard – cannellini beans, borlotti beans, chickpeas, broad (fava) beans, dried peas and lentils, as well as some local varieties. In the evening, after dinner, my elder sisters would check the beans or lentils for small stones and other impurities, rinse them well, place them in a large terracotta pot and cover them with water to soak overnight. In the morning, the water was drained and the pulses cooked in the same pot: terracotta was used for most of our slow-cooked dishes, as it not only enhanced the flavour of the food but also kept it warmer for longer. Beans and pulses are high in protein, and are so nutritious that they used to be known as 'poor man's meat'.

Nowadays, you can find all sorts of canned beans and pulses, which just need heating up, but I still love the ritual of handling the dried ones, putting them in water to soak and thinking of how to cook them. As well as retaining their texture and shape during cooking (the canned variety can get quite mushy), they taste far better. Once soaked, they are simply cooked in fresh water for an hour or so until tender (red kidney beans must be boiled hard for 10 minutes before the long simmering) and then you can use them according to your recipe. Sometimes I enjoy them as a dish in their own right, with some good extra virgin olive oil, garlic and herbs. So simple, so nutritious and so delicious.

## Cheap cuts of meat

The great thing about slow cooking is that you can use economical cuts of meat from different parts of the animal – lamb neck and shanks, pork belly and shoulder, beef chuck, shin and brisket, and offal such as tongue and oxtail, for example – rather than the tender cuts that are quick to cook but expensive. Although sometimes looked down upon, these cuts of meat make wonderful meals. When I was a child in Italy, no part of the animal was wasted, and this is still true in rural areas.

By slow cooking these tougher cuts, adding herbs and spices, you can produce a meal fit for a king, giving you maximum flavour for minimum effort while being kinder on your purse and respectful to the animal. Try the rustic mutton stew, *Montone alla contadina* (see page 98); pork in aspic jelly, *Liatina e' puorc* (see page 80); or the Sicilian-style pot-roasted beef flavoured with olives, almonds and cinnamon (see page 142). I've also come up with a simplified version of the Piedmontese dish *Bollito misto* (mixed boiled meats), using ox tongue, beef brisket and chicken rather than the traditional huge array of different meats (see page 76).

Game is fantastic for slow cooking too, and I consider myself lucky to have grown up in a family that loved to hunt. I learned not only how to hunt the animals, but also how to clean and cook them, and I still use my father's tips and recipes for rabbit, hare and pheasant. In season, I love to go out with friends on hunting trips and bring home whatever I catch. Pheasant makes a delicious ragù to serve with pasta, *Taglioni con ragù di fagiano in bianco* (see page 56), while the venison casserole, *Scottiglia di capriolo* (see page 104), can be used for almost any game, including wild boar, hare or rabbit.

## Kitchen kit

Slow cooking is comfort food at its best and easiest. Ask anyone what their favourite meal is, and you will very likely be told their mum's casserole, stew, roast or bake. With food, as with many other things in life, it's often the simple things that give the most pleasure and stay in our memories. Slow cooking goes back to basics: no major cooking skills or fancy gadgets are needed. A good, sturdy cooking pot or cast-iron casserole dish, ovenproof pans and roasting tins, plus a couple of wooden spoons, are all you really need.

A food processor or blender is undoubtedly useful, but when I was a child these items were almost unimaginable: whatever we cooked we did everything by hand, and there is always an alternative to modern gadgets – it will take longer, but the results will be just as good.

We didn't have electric slow cookers when I was a child and I still don't use one at home, preferring to use the old-fashioned stove-top. However, if you do have a slow cooker, you could use it for many of my recipes. With a slow cooker, once you've done the basic preparation you can leave the food to cook gently without worrying about things boiling dry. Cooking times are longer, so you need plenty of liquid, but you don't need to be in the kitchen to check the food as it cooks. We have included tips for recipes that work well in a slow cooker.

## One-pot cooking

Dishes that are cooked all in one pot, either on the stove-top or in the oven, are great for entertaining – and they can often be made in advance so all you have to do is reheat them when you have friends round. This way, you will have more time to relax, knowing that what you have made is cooked to perfection and you don't need to keep popping into the kitchen. One-pot dishes are also ideal for busy people. Set aside a little time to make a stew, pasta sauce or soup and freeze in batches for a quick, home-cooked meal at the end of the day. Try Lamb stew with butternut squash and saffron (see page 101); Boozy baked chicken with peppers, *Pollo ubriaco* (see page 152); the wonderful Italian classic slow-cooked beef or veal with onions, *La Genovese* (see page 42), to serve with pasta; or a summer vegetable stew, *Verdure estive stufate* (see page 108).

This book is about taking it slowly but surely, enjoying the simple things, learning how to make the most of a few basic ingredients and above all relaxing and enjoying good food – *buon appetito!*

## Slow food movement

The slow food movement is an organization which promotes locally-produced food and encourages traditional regional dishes. Started in Italy by Carlo Petrini as a backlash against the rising number of fast foods, it is now present in more than 150 countries worldwide.

The organization focuses on ensuring that food is produced using environmentally sustainable methods, without the use of synthetic chemicals, making food cleaner and healthier for all. It recognizes small, artisan producers promoting fair and ethical farming ensuring just wages and working conditions. Eating in season is encouraged, as is food quality rather than quantity.

Food traditions are highly respected and restaurants who adhere to working with sustainable produce as well as taking a "slower" approach to cooking are recognized and rewarded with the slow food snail logo. If you eat at such a restaurant, you can be assured that whatever you choose from the menu will be excellent.

The respect of food, choosing carefully what you buy, minimal waste and taking your time to cook from scratch, is the slow food philosophy I was brought up on – which unfortunately over time has been forgotten in favour of quick fixes and bad fast food. I am grateful to the slow food movement for its efforts in Italy and around the world to bring back the old traditions and sustainability we so desperately need in the food industry and at home.

# SOUPS

For me, soup is the ultimate comfort food. There is nothing so warming as returning home on cold winter evenings to a steaming bowl of homemade soup. Or at the weekend, after a walk in the woods, knowing you have a welcoming pot of soup waiting for you. You can make soup out of anything you like and it is an excellent way of using up leftovers. It can be made in advance and heated up when required, or made in large quantities and frozen in batches to be enjoyed when you have less time to cook. It is one of the simplest of foods, but always one of the most satisfying and pleasurable.

In Italy, soup – whether delicate or hearty – is popular and is sometimes served as a *primo* (first course) in place of pasta or risotto. Lunches in Italy are often substantial, so in the evening a lighter meal is preferred, and this is often just a broth made from homemade vegetable, chicken or beef stock with the addition of *pastina* (small pasta shapes).

I love making meat stock or broth: all the ingredients go into one large pot and cook slowly until the meat is tender; the resulting stock can be served as a soup or used as the basis for another soup or stew. The tender meat is ready to eat as a main course, or can be made into other dishes such as salads or meatballs. It's a great way to make the most of economical cuts of meat.

My favourite soups have always been hearty and substantial; beans, pulses and thickly sliced vegetables left gently bubbling on the stove, served with a slice of toasted country bread, a drizzle of good extra virgin olive oil and a sprinkling of grated Parmesan – heaven on a plate!

# Zuppa di piselli secchi con lattuga
## Split pea soup with lettuce

This lovely, old-fashioned soup dates from the time before frozen peas were available, and Italian housewives kept dried split peas to use when fresh peas were not in season. When cooked, their texture is quite dense, so to balance this I have kept the potatoes and pancetta in chunky pieces rather than blending the soup. However, if you prefer, you can blend it before you add the milk and egg yolk mixture at the end. The addition of lettuce gives the soup a pleasant contrasting freshness. Split peas don't normally need pre-soaking, but check the packet instructions.

Serves 4

300g/10½oz/1½ cups dried split peas
2 tbsp extra virgin olive oil
50g/1¾oz/4 tbsp butter
1 small onion, sliced
1 celery heart, sliced
85g/3oz pancetta, cubed
2 potatoes, cut into chunks
1 litre/1¾ pints/4 cups hot vegetable
  broth (see page 36)
500ml/18fl oz/2cups hot water
250g/9oz lettuce
225ml/8fl oz/scant 1 cup milk
2 egg yolks, beaten
grated Parmesan, to serve

Rinse the split peas in cold water, discarding any small stones or other impurities; set aside.

Heat the olive oil and half of the butter in a large saucepan on a medium heat. Add the onion, celery and pancetta and sweat for 5 minutes, until softened.

Stir in the potatoes and split peas, add the broth and water, cover with a lid and cook on a low heat for 1½ hours, stirring from time to time to prevent the peas from sticking.

About 15 minutes before the end of cooking time, put the lettuce leaves in a pan of boiling water and simmer for 6 minutes. Drain, squeezing out excess water, and leave to cool, then slice thinly lengthways. Set aside.

Melt the remaining butter and transfer to a bowl with the milk and egg yolks, whisking well. Remove the pea soup from the heat, stir in the milk mixture and serve sprinkled with the sliced lettuce and Parmesan.

# Minestra di verdure e riso

## Vegetable soup with rice

This is a lighter version of the classic minestrone vegetable soup, made with spring vegetables and rice instead of the usual pasta.

Serves 4

200g/7oz Swiss chard
3 tbsp extra virgin olive oil, plus
   extra to drizzle
60g/2¼oz pancetta, finely chopped
1 garlic clove, left whole
1 onion, sliced
1 celery stalk with leaves, sliced
1 carrot, cut into chunks
1 potato, cut into chunks
1 courgette (zucchini), cut into chunks
8 cherry tomatoes
100g/3½oz/⅔ cup fresh broad
  (fava) beans
a handful of basil leaves
salt and freshly ground black pepper
2 litres/3½ pints/2 quarts hot vegetable
  broth (see page 36)
100g/3½oz/½ cup arborio rice
grated Parmesan, to serve (optional)

Separate the white stalks of the Swiss chard from the green leaves; roughly chop the stalks and leaves and set aside.

Heat the olive oil in a large saucepan, add the pancetta, garlic, onion, celery and carrot and sweat on a medium heat for 4 minutes. Add the potato, courgette, tomatoes, chard stalks, broad beans, basil, salt and pepper, stir and cook for 1 minute.

Add the broth, increase the heat and bring to the boil, then reduce the heat, partially cover with the lid and cook for 50 minutes. Add the chard leaves and rice and continue to cook on a low heat for about 20 minutes, until the rice is al dente. If you need a little more liquid during cooking or when you add the rice, add more hot stock (or hot water).

Remove from the heat, taste for seasoning and serve in individual bowls with a drizzle of extra virgin olive oil and some grated Parmesan if desired.

# Minestra di ceci
## Chickpea soup

If you like chickpeas, you'll love this rustic soup, flavoured with pork rind (you may need to ask for this in advance from your butcher or supermarket); you can remove the rind before serving if you prefer. Put all the ingredients in a large pot and leave it to bubble gently on the stove, just like farmers' wives used to do in rural parts of Italy; when the family came home, there was always a warm bowl of soup ready and waiting. Remember to soak the chickpeas overnight the day before you make the soup.

Serves 4

500g/1lb 2oz/2½ cups dried
   chickpeas, soaked in water overnight
500g/1lb 2oz pork rind, sliced into
   12 x 3cm/4½ x 1-inch strips
2 onions, finely sliced
2 garlic cloves, left whole
4 large potatoes, peeled and left whole
1 tsp marjoram
10 basil leaves
5 tbsp extra virgin olive oil, plus
   extra to drizzle
freshly ground black pepper

Drain and rinse the chickpeas. Put them in a large saucepan together with all the remaining ingredients and 1 litre/1¾ pints/4 cups water. Bring to the boil, partially cover with a lid and cook on a low heat for 3–4 hours, or until the chickpeas are tender (the potatoes will break up and make the soup thicker). Serve with a drizzle of extra virgin olive oil.

# Brodo di carne

## Beef broth

When I make *brodo di carne* I always choose beef brisket, an inexpensive boneless cut from the breast of the animal. Brisket is one of the toughest cuts of beef and is perfect for slow cooking, gradually becoming tender and releasing its flavour. This is one of my favourite comfort foods, especially in cold weather. I like to cook some tortellini in the broth for a first course and then serve the boiled beef and vegetables as a main; or use the beef to make a salad (see page 70) or meatballs (see page 72). The beef broth can be made a couple of days in advance and kept in the fridge, leaving the meat and vegetables in the liquid. The beef broth can also be used as stock for soups and stews, and can be frozen.

Serves 4

1kg/2lb 4oz beef brisket
1 large onion
2 large carrots
2 celery stalks with leaves
3 turnips
3 bay leaves
6 black peppercorns
1 tsp salt

Put the meat in a large saucepan and add 3 litres/ 5¼ pints/3 quarts cold water, making sure the meat is covered – if necessary, add more water. Bring to the boil. You will notice scum appearing on the surface; remove this with a slotted spoon.

Add the rest of the ingredients, reduce the heat to low, cover with a lid and simmer very gently for 3 hours.

Remove the meat and vegetables from the pan and set aside. Strain the liquid through a fine sieve. To serve as a soup, pour the broth back into the pan and reheat, cooking some tortellini or small pasta shapes in the broth if you like. Slice the meat and cut the vegetables into chunks to serve after the broth.

# Brodo di pollo
## Chicken broth

For the best chicken broth, ask your butcher for a boiling chicken; in Italy this is called *gallina*, an older hen who has stopped laying eggs and is best used for making broth or stock. Otherwise, a normal roasting chicken will suffice. Chicken stock is used in many recipes, so it is worth making lots: you can freeze whatever you don't use, or even make a double quantity and freeze in batches. You can serve this as a light broth or a more substantial soup. Alternatively, this recipe makes a lovely two-course meal: you can have the broth with some *pastina* (small pasta shapes) or tortellini and then enjoy the chicken as a main course with the carrots and onion and some extra vegetables. The chicken can be eaten hot or cold; try it in a salad (see page 78).

Serves 4–6

1.5kg/3lb 5oz chicken
2 carrots
1 large onion
2 celery stalks with leaves
a handful of parsley
1 tsp sea salt
4 black peppercorns

Put all the ingredients in a large saucepan and add 3 litres/5¼ pints/3 quarts cold water, making sure the chicken is covered – if necessary add more water. Bring to the boil, then reduce the heat to low, cover with a lid and simmer gently for 2 hours.

Remove the chicken and vegetables from the pan and set aside. Strain the liquid through a fine sieve for a clear broth. Taste for seasoning and add a little more salt if necessary. To serve as a soup, pour the broth back into the pan and reheat, cooking some tortellini or small pasta shapes in the broth if you like. For a more substantial soup, add chopped cooked vegetables, shredded chicken and some pasta.

# Brodo di pollo con polpettine di pollo

## Chicken broth with chicken dumplings

This hearty soup is a delicious one-course meal – comfort food at its best. It's based on chicken broth (opposite); the cooked chicken is made into dumplings, which are then simmered in the broth.

Serves 4–6

chicken and broth from chicken broth
    recipe (opposite)
100g/3½oz country bread with crusts
    removed, very finely chopped
100g/3½oz Parmesan, grated, plus
    extra to serve
1 tbsp chives, finely snipped
salt and freshly ground black pepper
2 eggs

Remove the chicken skin and take all the flesh off the bones, breaking the flesh into pieces. Put the chicken in a food processor and whizz until minced (ground). Alternatively, chop it very finely with a sharp knife.

In a bowl, combine the chicken, bread, Parmesan, chives, salt and pepper to taste, and the eggs. Shape into balls about the size of walnuts and set aside.

Strain the broth into a large saucepan, bring to the boil, add the chicken dumplings and simmer on a medium heat for a couple of minutes. Remove from the heat and serve the broth in bowls with about four or five dumplings per person; sprinkle with a little grated Parmesan and black pepper if desired.

# Brodo 'e purpo
## Octopus broth

This dish was once typical of street food in Naples, and I have given its name in Neapolitan dialect. It is still eaten as street food but is not as common as it used to be. It is considered to be a winter dish, served with lots of black pepper and a squeeze of lemon juice, and often used as a cold remedy. You can enjoy the broth as a starter and serve the octopus as a main course salad (see page 82). You will need to order the octopus from your fishmonger.

Serves 4

1 whole octopus, weighing about
   1.2kg/2lb 10oz
1 tsp salt
4 bay leaves
15 black peppercorns
freshly ground black pepper, to serve
freshly squeezed lemon juice, to serve
   (optional)

Rinse the octopus under cold running water and set aside.

Put 1.5 litres/2½ pints/1½ quarts water, the salt, bay leaves and peppercorns into a large saucepan and bring to the boil. Hold the octopus by its head and dip it into the hot water several times – this is done to curl the tentacles. Put the octopus in the boiling water, cover with a lid and simmer on a medium–low heat for about 1¼ hours, until tender.

Carefully remove the octopus and set aside on a plate, together with a little of the broth; use to make Octopus salad (see page 82). Serve the broth in cups or bowls with lots of freshly ground black pepper and a drizzle of lemon juice, if desired.

# Zuppa di cipolle con fontina

## Onion soup with fontina cheese

A Tuscan version of onion soup, called *carabaccia*, which dates back to ancient times, includes cinnamon, almonds and basil. I have kept my onion soup simple, and to give it that extra Italian flavour I have used fontina cheese for the topping. The inclusion of white wine, and the slow cooking on a gentle heat, really brings out the taste of the onions. Easy to make, this nutritious and flavoursome soup is a welcome winter warmer.

Serves 4

1 bay leaf
3 sprigs of thyme
50g/1¾oz/4 tbsp butter
1.3kg/3lb onions, finely sliced
2 garlic cloves, left whole
30g/1oz/3 tbsp plain (all-purpose) flour
1 litre/1¾ pints/4 cups beef broth
   (see page 25)
400ml/14fl oz/1⅔ cups dry white wine
salt and freshly ground black pepper

**for the topping**
4 slices of ciabatta bread
150g/5½oz fontina cheese,
   finely chopped

Tie the herbs together and set aside.

Heat the butter in a large saucepan on a medium heat, add the onions, garlic and tied herbs and sweat for 5 minutes. Stir in the flour, whisking well to prevent lumps, then pour in the broth and wine. Add a pinch of salt and cook on a low heat, partially covered, for about 1¼ hours.

Preheat your grill (broiler) to hot. Remove the soup pan from the heat and discard the herbs and garlic. Divide the soup among four heatproof bowls, place a slice of ciabatta on top of each and sprinkle with the fontina.

Put the bowls of soup under the grill for 2 minutes, until the cheese melts and turns golden. Sprinkle with black pepper and serve at once.

Vg

# Zuppa di borlotti sul pane

## Borlotti bean and vegetable soup served on bread

Poor families traditionally served bean soup on bread to add bulk to the family meal. Sometimes the soup was poured into the empty cavity of bread rolls – the scooped-out bread being used for breadcrumbs or in other dishes. This is a nutritious recipe packed with vegetables, and the red onion added at the end gives the soup crunch. If you don't have borlotti beans, you can use cannellini.

Serves 4

250g/9oz/1¼ cups dried borlotti
   beans, soaked in water overnight
6 sage leaves
2 garlic cloves, left whole
4 tbsp extra virgin olive oil, plus
   extra to drizzle
2 carrots, sliced
2 celery stalks, sliced
400g/14oz ripe tomatoes, roughly
   chopped
140g/5oz chicory, roughly chopped
2 small leeks, sliced
100g/3½oz savoy cabbage, shredded
salt and freshly ground black pepper
1.2 litres/2 pints/5 cups hot water
1 tbsp chopped fresh parsley
4 slices of country bread, toasted
1 small red onion, thinly sliced

Drain the beans, rinse and put them in a large saucepan. Add the sage, garlic and enough water to cover the beans. Bring to the boil, then reduce the heat, cover with a lid and simmer for 1 hour, or until the beans are tender and cooked (check the packet instructions). Drain the beans and discard the garlic. Mash a quarter of the beans and set aside.

Heat the olive oil in a large saucepan on a medium heat, add the carrots, celery and tomatoes and sweat for a couple of minutes. Add the chicory, leeks and cabbage, season, cover with a lid and cook on a low heat for 15 minutes. Add the hot water and continue to cook for a further 15 minutes. Add the whole beans, mashed beans and parsley and continue to cook gently for 30 minutes.

Remove from the heat and taste for seasoning. Put a slice of toasted bread in each of four bowls and pour over the bean soup. Top with a few slices of red onion, drizzle with olive oil and serve.

Vg

# Zuppa di orzo e cavolo nero
## Pearl barley and cavolo nero soup

I love pearl barley and often use it in soups or as a substitute for rice. *Cavolo nero* is a loose-leafed Tuscan cabbage with very dark green, almost black, leaves – hence its Italian name, which translates as 'black cabbage'. As well as being tasty, both pearl barley and cavolo nero are very nutritious, and this easy-to-prepare soup is a complete meal in itself. Both ingredients can be found in good supermarkets.

Serves 4

150g/5½oz pearl barley
3 tbsp extra virgin olive oil, plus
   extra to drizzle
1 onion, finely chopped
400g/14oz cavolo nero, roughly chopped
1 large potato, peeled and cubed
115g/4oz tomatoes, chopped
1 litre/1¾ pints/4 cups vegetable broth
   (see page 36)
salt and freshly ground black pepper
4 slices of country bread, toasted, to
   serve (optional)

Rinse the barley and put it in a saucepan; add cold water to cover. Bring to the boil, then reduce the heat, cover with a lid and simmer for 1 hour, until the barley is cooked. Drain well and set aside.

Heat the olive oil in a large saucepan, add the onion and sweat for 5 minutes. Stir in the cavolo nero, potato and tomatoes. Add the cooked barley and the broth and season with salt and pepper. Bring to the boil, then reduce the heat to low, cover with a lid and cook for 40 minutes.

Remove from the heat, add a drizzle of olive oil and serve with toasted country bread.

Vg

# Zuppa di barbabietole e sedano rapa

## Beetroot and celeriac soup

These are two of my wife Liz's favourite vegetables, so she decided to combine them while testing recipes for this book. Wow, what a taste! And so simple to make; just put all the vegetables in a pot and leave to slow cook until tender, whizz and serve. Can be enjoyed at any time, but it's an elegant soup for a dinner party.

Serves 4

500g/1lb 2oz celeriac (celery root), peeled and cut into large chunks
150g/5½oz beetroot (beets), peeled and cut into large chunks
1 large potato, peeled and cut into large chunks
1 celery stalk with leaves, roughly chopped
1 onion, roughly chopped
1.3 litres/2¼ pints/5½ cups vegetable broth (see page 36)
salt and freshly ground black pepper
a handful of parsley, finely chopped
natural yogurt, to serve (optional)

Put all the vegetables in a large saucepan together with the broth, bring to the boil, then reduce the heat, partially cover with a lid and simmer gently for 1 hour, until tender.

Remove from the heat and blend until smooth. Add salt and pepper to taste. Serve in individual bowls, sprinkled with parsley and a swirl of yogurt if desired.

Vg

# Brodo di verdure
## Vegetable broth

Vegetable broth or stock is at the base of many traditional Italian dishes – risotto, soups and stews – or it can simply be served as a soup. Ready-made stock can be very good, but nothing beats the fresh flavour of your own homemade broth, made with the freshest of vegetables. It is worth making a double quantity and freezing in batches. Being the lightest of all broths, it is popular for weaning babies or if you are feeling fragile, possibly with the addition of some tortellini or pastina (small pasta shapes). Or you can simply drink it as it is!

Serves 4

1 onion, peeled
1 courgette (zucchini)
1 carrot
1 celery stalk with leaves
1 leek
1 potato, peeled
2 cherry tomatoes
a handful of parsley, including stalks
2 tbsp extra virgin olive oil
1 tsp sea salt

Put all the ingredients in a large saucepan, add 1.5 litres/2½ pints/1½ quarts water and bring to the boil. Reduce the heat, cover with a lid and simmer gently for 1¼ hours. Taste for seasoning and add more salt if necessary.

Remove from the heat and strain the broth through a fine sieve, pressing down well on the vegetables with the back of a spoon. Serve hot, or reheat, adding some small pasta shapes to cook in the broth if you like.

# Vg

# Minestrone invernale vegano
## Vegan winter minestrone

This classic Italian vegetable soup never disappoints and makes a wonderful hearty, nutritious meal at any time. My version uses lots of winter root veggies, but you can swap out any of the ingredients according to the season and what you have to hand. I like my vegetables quite chunky and use broken-up spaghetti, but you can use any small pasta shapes as well as using cannellini or other beans in place of the traditional borlotti. For non-vegans and non-vegetarians, add a sprinkling of grated Parmesan to serve.

Serves 8

100g/3½oz/½ cup dried borlotti beans, soaked in water overnight
5 tbsp extra virgin olive oil, plus extra for drizzling
1 large onion, chopped
2 celery stalks and leaves, chopped
2 carrots, chopped
1 leek, chopped
1 parsnip, cubed
200g/7oz celeriac (cleaned weight), cubed
200g/7oz pumpkin flesh, cubed
1 small cauliflower, broken up into florets
2 potatoes, cubed
200g/7oz savoy or sweetheart cabbage, roughly chopped
1.7 litres/57fl oz/scant 7 cups hot vegetable stock (see page 36) – or use a stock cube
1 tbsp tomato purée (paste), diluted with a little of the hot veg stock
100g/3½oz/scant ½ cup dried spaghetti, broken-up
salt & freshly ground black pepper
rustic bread, to serve

Drain the soaked borlotti beans and place in a saucepan, covered with fresh cold water. Bring to the boil, lower the heat and cook for about 50 minutes, until soft (check cooking instructions on your packet for timings.)

Once cooked, remove from the heat and set aside, including the cooking liquid.

Heat the olive oil in a large pot and sweat the onion, celery, carrots, leek, parsnip, celeriac and pumpkin on a medium heat for 10 minutes.

Stir in the cauliflower and potatoes, then continue to sweat them down. After a couple of minutes, stir in the cabbage, beans, cooking liquid, stock and tomato purée. Bring to the boil, then simmer gently, partially covered with a lid, for 25 minutes, until the vegetables are tender.

Increase the heat, bring to the boil and stir in the broken-up spaghetti. Continue to cook on a medium-low heat for about 10 minutes, until the pasta is cooked.

Check the seasoning and, if necessary, add some salt and pepper to taste.

Remove the soup from the heat and serve in bowls, along with rustic bread and a drizzle of olive oil.

# PASTA

—

Pasta is the best-loved dish of all Italians and its popularity has spread worldwide – no wonder, as it makes a satisfying meal and many pasta dishes are quick to cook. However, there are lots of sauces and baked pasta dishes that require long, slow cooking. One of the best examples has to be ragù: there are many variations of ragù, but all are based on the principle of meat or other ingredients cooked very slowly so that they become superbly tender and their flavour creates a wonderful sauce. During hunting season, I will use whatever I have caught – perhaps pheasant, pigeon, hare or rabbit – cooked slowly to make a deliciously rich sauce to serve with pappardelle or tagliatelle.

My family's slow-cooked ragù, which we enjoyed for Sunday lunches, would take at least 12 hours to cook. My zia (aunt) Maria was the expert and she would start her ragù on Saturday and leave it to cook very, very gently on the smallest of flames on the stove all through the night for a ragù that was cooked to absolute perfection – the meat so tender and crumbly and the dense sauce with its unforgettable consistency and taste.

I love pasta dishes that can be served as two courses, such as the southern Italian ragù (see page 44) and La Genovese (see page 42), where a large piece of meat is cooked slowly and the resulting sauce is served with pasta as a first course followed by the meat as a main. These are some of my favourite dishes to cook, especially when I have a crowd for dinner. Not only are they simple to prepare, they go a long way and you know they will please everyone!

When I was growing up in southern Italy, pasta al forno, or baked pasta, was a must for special occasions like Christmas, weddings and christenings. At these times, the wood fire would be lit well in advance and large terracotta dishes would be baked for hours. A lasagne made with tomato sauce, meatballs, boiled eggs and lots of local salami and cheese was a sure favourite at these grand occasions. Baked pasta dishes can be made in advance and slowly cooked in the oven, and they don't mind waiting around before you serve them. They are ever-popular for Sunday lunches, at parties, or when you have lots of people round.

—

# La Genovese con pennette
## Slow-cooked onion sauce with pasta, followed by veal

Although the title suggests otherwise, this is a Neapolitan classic and, like ragù, is a Sunday lunch favourite in the Campania region. The recipe has age-old roots and there are various stories about its origins. One says it was prepared in *osterie* (inns) at the port of Naples by cooks from Genova for Genovese sailors. Large pieces of meat were slow-cooked with onions in order to create a flavoursome pasta sauce and a main course to feed the hungry sailors. Nowadays everyone has their own version. Beef is commonly used, but I prefer the milder taste of veal, which marries well with the onions; after long, gentle cooking these become sweet, with a meltingly soft texture that is perfect for a pasta sauce.

Serves 4

800g/1lb 12oz veal joint
salt and freshly ground black pepper
2 garlic cloves, sliced
100ml/3½fl oz/scant ½ cup extra
    virgin olive oil
2.5kg/5lb 8oz large onions, sliced
1 celery stalk, finely chopped
1 large carrot, finely chopped
85g/3oz salami, finely chopped
3 sage leaves
1 sprig of rosemary
2 bay leaves
200ml/7fl oz/scant 1 cup dry
    white wine
350g/12oz pennette pasta
30g/1oz pecorino (romano)
    cheese, grated

Rub the veal all over with salt and pepper, make some incisions in the meat and poke in the garlic slices.

Heat the olive oil in a large saucepan on a medium heat. Add the veal and brown well all over. Remove from the pan and set aside.

Add the onions, celery, carrot, salami and herbs, season with salt and pepper and sweat for about 30 minutes on a low heat.

Put the meat back in the pan, add the wine and allow to evaporate. Reduce the heat to very low, cover with a lid and cook for 3 hours, until the meat is very tender. Check from time to time to make sure it isn't sticking to the pan, turning the meat and stirring the onions.

Remove the meat from the pan and set aside. Using a potato masher, mash the onions slightly and taste for seasoning.

Cook the pennette in lightly salted boiling water until al dente, drain and toss with the onions. Serve with grated pecorino cheese and freshly ground black pepper. Slice the veal and serve as a main course with a green salad.

# Il ragù antico

## Slow-cooked ragù

*Simbolo della domenica in famiglia* ('the symbol of Sunday with the family')

This dish is a very popular and traditional Sunday lunch in most southern Italian families. When I was growing up, Sunday just wasn't Sunday without *il ragù*. The weekend would traditionally begin with the housewife's early trip to the butcher to obtain the perfect cuts of meat; with the package firmly clutched under her arm, she would begin to imagine how it would be cooked. Once at home, surrounded by children, grandparents and the odd neighbour or two, she would begin preparations for this weekly ritual – discussions would erupt among the women as to what should go in, how the meat should be sealed and so on. Just like in the film *Saturday, Sunday and Monday* (1990), when Sophia Loren goes to the butcher and ends up in a fiery discussion with other housewives as to what makes the perfect ragù! Ultimately, the ragù would be left slowly, slowly bubbling away on the stove, in a large terracotta pot, for most of Saturday and sometimes even throughout the night – a cooking time of 12 hours or more was quite normal. As the ragù gently simmered, the women went about making fresh pasta and gossiping, or in some families the rosary was recited. The smell of the bubbling ragù, the warmth from the wood-fired stove, the squeals of playing children and the animated voices of the women gave the serene feeling of home, family and the sign that the weekend was truly under way.

Traditionally the ragù was made with various cuts of beef – shin, knuckle, chuck – with the precious addition of *nervetti* (tendons) to give more flavour, as well as cuts of pork such as ribs and shanks. Home-preserved bottled tomatoes, made at the end of summer, gave the ragù its unique taste.

The secret to simmering a perfect ragù is to put it on an extremely low heat, partially cover the pot and listen for that gentle 'plop, plop, plop' sound during cooking. When the sauce and olive oil separate and the oil comes to the top, you know the ragù is ready.

The ragù is enjoyed as two courses, the first course being the rich tomato sauce served with pasta, followed by the meat. Pasta shapes such as *ziti* or candele were popular, but this varied from village to village; in my home village, Minori, we preferred *fusilli*. Not the mass-produced twist shapes found in the shops today, but long, thin curls made by rolling the pasta around umbrella spokes. I know ladies who still make *fusilli* like this today and when I go back to visit, I make sure I bring back a bagful to enjoy with my version of *il ragù*.

Serves 4–6

3 tbsp extra virgin olive oil
1 onion, finely chopped
600g/1lb 5oz beef shin, cut into
    about six chunks
4 pork ribs
500g/1lb 2oz stewing pork, cut
    into chunks
75ml/2½fl oz/5 tbsp red wine
1 tbsp tomato purée (paste), mixed
    with 1 tbsp lukewarm water
400g/14oz can chopped tomatoes
500ml/18fl oz/2 cups tomato passata
    (strained tomatoes)
a handful of basil leaves
salt and freshly ground black pepper

Heat the olive oil in a very large saucepan, add the onion and sweat for a couple of minutes on a medium heat. Add all the meat and brown well all over.

Add the wine and allow to evaporate. Then add the tomato purée and stir to coat the meat. Add the canned tomatoes and cook for a minute, then add the passata, basil, salt and pepper. Bring to the boil, then reduce the heat to very, very low, partially cover with a lid and cook for 6 hours. Check the liquid level (top up with a little stock or water if necessary) and stir very carefully from time to time.

After 3 hours, remove the ribs and pork and set aside.

About 20 minutes before the end of cooking time, return the ribs and pork to the sauce to heat through.

Remove the pan from the heat and leave to rest for 10 minutes. Using a slotted spoon, remove the meat and set aside. Use the tomato sauce to dress freshly cooked pasta and serve the meat as a main course.

## For a slow cooker

Traditionally this is always cooked in a large pot, and all the meat is browned together so the flavours begin to mingle. When using a slow cooker you may find it easier to brown the meat in batches.

Sweat the onion and brown the meat as above. Continue as above and bring to the boil, then transfer everything to a large slow cooker pot, press the meat beneath the liquid, cover and cook on Low for 8–9 hours (there's no need to remove the ribs and pork from the slow cooker). Serve as above.

# Ragù Bolognese

## Classic Bolognese ragù

Although one of the most popular pasta sauces worldwide, the Bolognese is so often made badly outside of Italy: too much tomato, not cooked for long enough and usually served with spaghetti, hence the term 'spag bol' - unheard of in Italy! Because of all these differences and others, the Bolognese association of the *Accademia Italiana della Cucina* decided in 1982 to declare an official recipe. Although the original recipe used a whole cut of meat which was cut into tiny pieces, the *Accademia* allows for minced meat for ease of preparation. Only double- or triple-concentrated tomato purée is used (the kind sold in tubes in the supermarket is usually double-concentrated) and the addition of milk towards the end of cooking takes away any acidity from the tomato. The thick meat sauce would fall off the thin strands of spaghetti and so the Bolognese always serve it with tagliatelle; this ragù is also used for lasagne. For a rich, dense sauce, slow-cook for at least 2 hours. It is always worth making more than you need so you can freeze some in batches.

Serves 4

3 tbsp extra virgin olive oil
30g/1oz butter
1 onion, finely chopped
1 celery stalk, finely chopped
1 carrot, finely chopped
150g/5½oz pancetta, cubed
200g/7oz minced (ground) beef
200g/7oz minced (ground) pork
200ml/7fl oz/scant 1 cup red wine
1½ tbsp tomato purée (paste)
200ml/7fl oz/scant 1 cup beef stock
   (see page 25) – or use a stock cube
100ml/3½fl oz/scant ½ cup full-fat milk

Heat the olive oil and butter in a large saucepan, add the onion, celery, carrot and pancetta and sweat on a gentle heat for about 10 minutes, until the onion has softened.

Add the meat and brown all over. Increase the heat, add the wine and allow to evaporate. Dilute the tomato purée in a little of the stock and stir into the meat. Reduce the heat to low, cover with a lid and cook on a gentle heat for 2 hours, checking and adding a little extra stock from time to time to prevent the sauce from drying out.

About 10 minutes before the end of cooking time, stir in the milk.

Serve with freshly cooked tagliatelle.

### For a slow cooker

Sweat the vegetables and pancetta and brown the meat as above. Add the wine and allow to evaporate, then dilute the tomato purée in 350ml/12fl oz/1½ cups stock, bring to the boil and transfer to a medium slow cooker pot. Cover and cook on Low for 8–9 hours. Stir in the milk and cook for 10 minutes. Serve as above.

For a large slow cooker pot, make double the quantity: cooking times remain the same.

# Tagliatelle con ragù d'agnello in bianco con finocchietto

## Tagliatelle with lamb and wild fennel

When we talk about ragù, we tend to think of the traditional sauce made with beef and tomatoes. This is a much lighter version, made *in bianco* ('in the white' – as Italians refer to dishes not cooked in tomato sauce). Italians tend to eat this dish in the spring, when lamb is at its best and wild fennel is found in abundance. Rather than using minced (ground) lamb, I use a piece of lamb cut into small bite-size pieces, keeping its texture, and slow-cook it on a gentle heat. The simple combination of lamb, wild fennel and a sprinkling of pecorino is delicious.

Serves 4

4 tbsp extra virgin olive oil
1 onion, finely sliced
1 celery stalk, finely sliced
400g/14oz lamb, cut into small pieces
100ml/3½fl oz/scant ½ cup dry
    white wine
salt and freshly ground black pepper
a handful of wild fennel, roughly
    chopped
300ml/10fl oz/1¼ cups vegetable stock
    (see page 36) – or use a stock cube
325g/11½oz dried tagliatelle pasta
40g/1½oz pecorino (romano)
    cheese, grated

Heat the olive oil in a large saucepan, add the onion and celery and sweat on a low heat for 20 minutes, stirring from time to time, until softened.

Increase the heat, add the lamb and brown well all over. Add the wine and allow to evaporate. Season and add a couple of fennel sprigs and 100ml/3½fl oz/scant ½ cup of the stock. Reduce the heat to very low, cover with a lid and cook for 1 hour, checking from time to time and gradually adding a little more of the stock. After about 55 minutes, stir in the remaining fennel.

When almost ready to serve, bring a large saucepan of lightly salted water to the boil and cook the tagliatelle until al dente. Drain, reserving a little of the cooking water. Add the pasta and a couple of tablespoons of the cooking water to the sauce and mix well. Remove from the heat, sprinkle with the pecorino and serve.

Vg

# Ragù vegano di lenticchie
## Vegan lentil 'Bolognese'

Lentils are the perfect alternative to meat in a traditional Bolognese sauce. Simple to prepare with a few basic ingredients, this makes a wonderful hearty, nutritious meal. Pappardelle pasta goes really well with ragù sauces, but you could use tagliatelle, penne, farfalle or any pasta shape that you prefer. For extra bulk and flavour, I have added pumpkin and mushrooms, but you could swap them out with other veggies or omit altogether for a simpler sauce – always remembering the basic soffritto ingredients of onion, celery and carrot.

Serves 6

280g/10oz/scant 1½ cups dried
   brown or green lentils
5 tbsp extra virgin olive oil, plus
   extra for drizzling
1 small onion, finely chopped
1 celery stalk, finely chopped
1 small carrot, finely chopped
100g/3½oz/scant ½ cup pumpkin
   flesh, finely chopped
2 garlic cloves, whole, peeled
   and crushed
200g/7oz/scant ¼ cup chestnut
   button mushrooms, thinly sliced
2 bay leaves
400ml/14fl oz/1¾ cups tomato
   passata (strained tomatoes)
900ml/31fl oz/3½ cups hot vegetable
   stock (see page 36) – or use a
   stock cube
500g/1lb 2oz/scant 4 cups dried
   egg-free pappardelle pasta
salt
rustic bread, to serve (optional)
chilli flakes, to serve (optional)

Rinse the lentils under plenty of cold water, checking for any impurities.

Heat the olive oil in a pan, then sweat the onion, celery, carrot, pumpkin and garlic on a medium heat for a couple of minutes. Stir in the lentils, mushrooms and bay leaves and cook for a couple of minutes.

Add the passata and stock, bring to the boil, then lower the heat and gently simmer for about 1 hour, until the lentils are cooked. You may need more or less stock depending on the type of lentils, so add this gradually.

Near the end of the cooking time, bring a large pot of salted water to the boil and cook the pasta until 'al dente'. Using tongs, transfer the pasta to the lentil ragù, mixing well and adding a little of the hot pasta water to loosen the sauce.

Remove from the heat and serve with rustic bread, a drizzle of olive oil and some chilli flakes, if desired.

# Maltagliati con cannellini e olive
## Fresh pasta strips with cannellini beans and olives

I love cannellini beans, especially the dried beans that need to be soaked overnight. Once the beans are soaked, this dish is really easy to make, and the beans and prosciutto give a wonderful aroma as they cook together. The addition of fresh crunchy celery, olives and tomatoes makes this fresher and lighter than a typical *pasta e fagioli* (pasta and beans) dish. Delicious served next day and can also be enjoyed cold.

Serves 4

300g/10½oz/1½ cups dried cannellini beans, soaked in water overnight
200g/7oz piece of prosciutto, cubed
1 celery stalk, finely chopped
20 green olives, finely chopped
2 tomatoes, deseeded and finely chopped
leaves from 2 sprigs of rosemary, finely chopped
1 garlic clove, finely chopped
4 tbsp extra virgin olive oil, plus extra to drizzle
300g/10½oz fresh pappardelle, roughlychopped into 10cm/4-inch long strips
30g/1oz Parmesan, grated, plus extra, shaved, to serve (optional)
a small handful of basil leaves, torn if large
salt and freshly ground black pepper

Rinse the beans and put them in a large saucepan with the prosciutto; add 2 litres/3½ pints/2 quarts cold water and bring to the boil. Reduce the heat, partially cover with a lid and cook on a very low heat for 1 hour, or until the beans are tender but not falling apart.

Combine the celery, olives, tomatoes, rosemary, garlic and olive oil and add to the beans. Increase the heat, bring to the boil and add the pasta, then reduce the heat to medium and cook for 2–3 minutes, until the pasta is al dente. Remove from the heat, stir in the Parmesan and basil, taste for seasoning and leave to rest for 5 minutes. Serve with black pepper, a drizzle of extra virgin olive oil and a few Parmesan shavings, if you like.

# Pappardelle con sugo di lepre

## Pappardelle with hare sauce

Hare meat is rich and dark like beef or venison. If you are a hunter yourself, you know how rare it is to catch a hare, but if you do get the chance or can buy hare from a good butcher, then I urge you to try this dish. The recipe was created by one of my chefs, Davide Bargione, who, like me, loves hare. The sauce can be made in advance and reheated.

Serves 6

1 hare, cut into 12 pieces
salt and freshly ground black pepper
500g/1lb 2oz fresh or dried pappardelle
grated Parmesan, to serve (optional)

**for the marinade**

1 litre/1¾ pints/4 cups red wine
150ml/5fl oz/⅔ cup white wine vinegar
1 garlic head, cloves separated
 and crushed
2 cinnamon sticks
1 tsp fennel seeds, lightly crushed
20 black peppercorns, lightly crushed
3 sprigs of rosemary
6 bay leaves
juice of 1 lemon
2 large celery stalks, roughly chopped
2 onions, roughly chopped

**for the sauce**

3 tbsp extra virgin olive oil
1 onion, finely chopped
2 celery stalks, finely chopped
1 carrot, finely chopped
bouquet garni of thyme, bay leaf,
 rosemary and parsley
2 tbsp tomato purée (paste)
200ml/7fl oz/scant 1 cup red wine
1.2kg/2lb 10oz (3 x 400g/14oz cans)
 canned chopped tomatoes
500ml/18fl oz/2 cups hot vegetable stock
 (see page 36) – or use a stock cube

Wash the hare thoroughly under cold running water and pat dry with kitchen paper. Put the hare in a large bowl together with the rest of the marinade ingredients, cover with clingfilm (plastic wrap) and leave in the fridge for at least 12 hours.

Remove the hare from the marinade, pat dry and season with salt and pepper. To make the sauce, heat the olive oil in a large saucepan and brown the hare all over. Remove the meat and set aside. In the same pan, sweat the onion, celery, carrot and bouquet garni together with the vegetables, garlic and herbs from the marinade for about 3 minutes. Stir in the tomato purée, add the wine and allow to evaporate. Return the hare to the pan, add the tomatoes, stock, some salt and pepper, and bring to the boil. Reduce the heat, cover with a lid and cook gently for 1½ hours.

At the end of the cooking time, remove the chunks of meat and set aside until cool enough to handle. Remove the meat from the bones, discard the bones, chop the meat finely and return to the sauce and heat through.

Meanwhile, bring a large saucepan of lightly salted water to the boil and cook the pappardelle until al dente. Drain, mix with the hare sauce and serve immediately, with a little grated Parmesan if desired.

# Tagliolini con ragù di fagiano in bianco

## Tagliolini with pheasant

This is one of my favourite dishes after a morning's shooting; I love getting together with all the other hunters and tucking into this tasty pasta dish. I often don't bother to marinate the pheasant, as I like the gamey flavour. As the sauce is *in bianco* ('white', or without tomato) the dish is quite light and shows off the full flavour of the meat. The sauce can be made in advance and reheated thoroughly before adding the pasta.

Serves 4

1 pheasant, cleaned, boned and cut into chunks (ask your butcher to do this)
salt and freshly ground black pepper
plain (all-purpose) flour, to dust
5 tbsp extra virgin olive oil
100ml/3½fl oz/scant ½ cup dry white wine
1 onion, finely chopped
1 celery stalk, finely chopped
1 carrot, finely chopped
1 sprig of rosemary
350ml/12fl oz/1½ cups hot vegetable stock (see page 36) – or use a stock cube
350g/12oz fresh or dried tagliolini pasta

**for the marinade**
400ml/14fl oz/1⅔ cups dry white wine
½ onion, roughly chopped
1 celery stalk, roughly chopped
1 carrot, roughly chopped
1 sprig of rosemary

Put the chunks of pheasant in a bowl together with all the marinade ingredients, cover with clingfilm (plastic wrap) and leave in the fridge overnight.

Remove the meat from the marinade, carefully remove the skin and discard. Dry the meat with kitchen paper, season with salt and pepper and dust with flour. Discard the marinade.

Heat half of the olive oil in a frying pan on a medium–high heat, add the pheasant and brown well all over, then add the wine and allow to evaporate.

In another frying pan, heat the remaining olive oil and sweat the onion, celery, carrot and rosemary until the vegetables have softened. Add the browned meat to the vegetables and mix together. Add the stock, some salt and pepper and bring to the boil, then reduce the heat, cover with a lid and cook gently for 50 minutes. Check from time to time and if necessary add more hot stock.

When almost ready to serve, cook the tagliolini in lightly salted boiling water until al dente. Drain, reserving a little of the cooking water, and add the pasta to the pheasant sauce, then toss well with a few tablespoons of the cooking water. Serve immediately.

# Paccheri con sugo di coniglio
## Paccheri with rabbit sauce

Paccheri are a traditional Neapolitan pasta in the shape of large, round tubes, which marry very well with a thick sauce like this. The sauce can be made in advance and reheated thoroughly before adding the pasta. Rabbit is quite a bland meat so it needs to be livened up with spices or herbs: here I've inserted cloves into an onion, which gives the sauce a spicy taste. This is a simple one-pot meal that will give you two courses: the pasta is served with the sauce as a starter and the rabbit follows as a main course, perhaps served with a green salad.

Serves 4

3 cloves
1 onion, peeled, left whole
4 tbsp extra virgin olive oil
1 carrot, finely chopped
1 garlic clove, left whole
½ red chilli, finely chopped
2 sage leaves
1kg/2lb 4oz rabbit, cut into chunks
   on the bone
750ml/1¼ pints/3 cups tomato
   passata(strained tomatoes)
salt
350g/12oz paccheri or lumaconi
   (large shells) pasta
grated pecorino (romano) cheese,
   to serve

Insert the cloves into the onion. Heat the olive oil in a large saucepan on a medium–high heat, add the onion, carrot, garlic, chilli and sage leaves and stir-fry until golden. Remove and discard the garlic. Add the rabbit and brown on all sides. Stir in the passata and some salt, reduce the heat, cover with a lid and simmer gently for 2 hours.

Remove the rabbit pieces and set aside. Strain the sauce and put it back in the saucepan to keep it warm, together with the rabbit.

Meanwhile, cook the paccheri in plenty of lightly salted boiling water until al dente. Drain, add to the sauce, mix well and serve with freshly grated pecorino cheese.

# Lasagne con ragù di verdure

## Lasagne with slow-cooked vegetable ragù

This is a lighter version of the classic lasagne, with vegetables replacing the meat Bolognese ragù. The vegetables are cooked on a very low heat so they do not go mushy and the flavours infuse well.

Serves 4

3 tbsp extra virgin olive oil
1 shallot, finely sliced
1 leek, finely sliced
1 celery stalk, finely sliced
1 carrot, finely sliced
1 turnip, finely sliced
150g/5½oz pumpkin, cubed
85g/3oz mushrooms, sliced
100g/3½oz curly endive,
    roughly chopped
1 garlic clove, crushed
1 sprig of marjoram
1 sprig of thyme
salt and freshly ground black pepper
3 tbsp canned chopped tomatoes
250ml/9fl oz/1 cup vegetable stock
    (see page 36) – or use a stock cube
butter, to grease and finish
8–10 fresh lasagne sheets
100g/3½oz Parmesan, grated

**for the white sauce**
40g/1½oz/3 tbsp butter
40g/1½oz/5 tbsp plain
    (all-purpose) flour
500ml/18fl oz/2 cups full-fat milk
a pinch of freshly grated nutmeg

Heat the olive oil in a large saucepan, add the shallot and leek and sweat on a medium heat for 3 minutes. Add the celery, carrot, turnip, pumpkin, mushrooms, endive, garlic, herbs and black pepper. Stir in the tomatoes and stock, reduce the heat to minimum, then cover with a lid and cook for 1½ hours, stirring from time to time.

Preheat the oven to 200°C/400°F/gas mark 6.

To make the sauce, melt the butter in a saucepan, remove from the heat and whisk in the flour very quickly to avoid lumps, then gradually add the milk, whisking well. Return to the heat and cook on a medium heat for 3–4 minutes, whisking all the time until the sauce begins to thicken. Remove from the heat and stir in some salt, pepper and nutmeg.

Grease an ovenproof dish, about 20 x 25cm/8 x 10 inches, with butter and spread a little of the white sauce on the bottom. Arrange a layer of lasagne sheets on top, followed by some vegetable ragù, a little white sauce, and a sprinkling of grated Parmesan. Continue making layers like this until you have used all the ingredients, ending with white sauce and grated Parmesan. Top with small knobs of butter. Cover with foil and bake in the oven for 20 minutes.

Remove the foil and cook for another 10 minutes to brown the top. Remove from the oven and leave to rest for 5 minutes before serving.

# Pasta e patate arraganate al forno

## Baked pasta and potatoes

My sister, Adriana, makes this dish; it is a cross between *pasta e patate* (pasta and potatoes), which was a much-loved dish in our family, and *patate arraganate* (sliced potatoes baked in the oven with oregano and tomatoes). It's a thrifty way to use up small amounts of dried pasta from your store cupboard, making a tasty, nutritious meal for a family midweek supper.

Serves 4

500g/1lb 2oz potatoes, cut into chunks
60g/2¼oz Parmesan: 30g/1oz roughly
   cut into cubes; 30g/1oz grated
250g/9oz dried pasta, broken up

**for the sauce**
1 tbsp extra virgin olive oil
1 onion, roughly chopped
1 celery stalk with leaves,
   roughly chopped
600g/1lb 5oz canned chopped tomatoes
a handful of fresh basil leaves, plus
   extra to serve
a pinch of dried oregano
salt and freshly ground black pepper

First, make the sauce: heat the olive oil in a saucepan and sweat the onion and celery for a couple of minutes. Add the tomatoes, then rinse out the can with 200ml/7fl oz/scant 1 cup water and add to the pan. Stir in the basil, oregano, salt and pepper and cook on a medium heat for 25 minutes.

Meanwhile, preheat the oven to 180°C/350°F/gas mark 4.

Put the tomato sauce and potatoes in an ovenproof dish about 20 x 25cm/8 x 10 inches, dot with pieces of Parmesan, cover with foil and bake for 45 minutes.

Cook the pasta in plenty of salted boiling water for 2 minutes, then drain, reserving about 200ml/7fl oz/scant 1 cup of the cooking water. Add the pasta to the sauce and potatoes, together with the reserved pasta cooking water. Sprinkle with grated Parmesan and scatter over a few basil leaves, then return to the oven for 15 minutes, without the foil. Remove from the oven and leave to rest for 5 minutes before serving.

# V

# Pasta e fagioli
## Pasta and beans

This dish is popular throughout Italy and each region, town, village and family have their own versions. The dish was a staple in most rural homes, slowly bubbling away in large terracotta pots over the ash of the fireplace to provide a warm, nutritious meal when the family returned home from a hard day working in the fields. This particular recipe is typical of the Abruzzo region, where it is normally made with fresh eggless tagliatelle-type pasta. *Pasta e fagioli* dishes are not traditionally served with grated cheese, but if you prefer you can grate some Parmesan or pecorino to sprinkle on when serving.

Serves 4

250g/9oz/1¼ cups dried borlotti
   beans, soaked in water overnight
3 tbsp extra virgin olive oil, plus
   extra to drizzle
½ onion, finely chopped
1 celery stalk, finely chopped
1 small carrot, finely chopped
½ red chilli, finely chopped (optional)
400g/14oz can chopped tomatoes
150g/5½oz tomato passata
   (strained tomatoes)
salt and freshly ground black pepper
250g/9oz dried tagliatelle, broken up

Drain and rinse the beans, put them in a saucepan with enough cold water to cover and bring to the boil. Reduce the heat to low, partially cover with a lid and cook for about 1 hour, or until the beans are tender. Drain, reserving a couple of tablespoons of the cooking water. Take about a quarter of the beans and mash them with the cooking water. Set aside.

Heat the olive oil in a saucepan, sweat the onion, celery, carrot and chilli, if using, for a couple of minutes, then add all the tomatoes, salt and pepper and cook on a medium heat, partially covered with a lid, for 20 minutes. Add all the beans and the reserved cooking water and continue to cook for 10 minutes, stirring from time to time.

Meanwhile, bring a large saucepan of lightly salted water to the boil and cook the tagliatelle until al dente. Drain, reserving a little of the cooking water, and add to the sauce, mixing well together; if necessary add a little of the cooking water. Remove from the heat and leave to rest for 5 minutes, then serve in individual bowls with a drizzle of extra virgin olive oil.

# LIGHT
# DISHES
# &
# LEFTOVERS

———

'Slow cooking' conjures up images of heavy meals for colder months, but the idea of taking things slowly can also create light, fresh-tasting dishes for snacks and summer eating.

Marinating is a form of 'slow cooking' that doesn't need the stove or oven, but it does need several hours for the flavours to mingle and marry. It's a simple technique with stunning results: as the food absorbs the flavourings, the taste improves. The dishes are enjoyed cold as an antipasto, snack or light but satisfying meal and can include all sorts of ingredients, from pumpkin in the *antipasto di zucca* to mackerel marinated with mint, and rabbit in a Tuscan salad.

While writing and testing recipes for this book, I encountered lots of slow-cooked dishes that could effortlessly be made into other meals. Once you've made a beef or chicken broth, for example, you can transform the main ingredient into another course or a meal for another day. Boiled beef can be transformed into a salad, meatballs or even burgers. Boiled chicken also makes a delicious salad. When I was brought up, food was never wasted and I still maintain those values. My sister Adriana is a genius at this and comes up with some amazing dishes using leftovers that most people would bin! Not only is it part of our culture never to waste food, but it also makes cooking a fun and imaginative process.

———

# Vg

# Antipasto di zucca arrostita marinata
## Pumpkin antipasto

This lovely roasted pumpkin makes an ideal antipasto served alongside some Parma ham and lots of good bread or crostini. The vinegar marinade gives the pumpkin a 'kick' and gets your taste buds going. This can be rustic or more elegant: marinate the pumpkin in four small ramekins and turn out onto serving plates. It can be made the day before and left in the fridge overnight – but serve at room temperature.

Serves 4

extra virgin olive oil, to grease
   and drizzle
850g/1lb 14oz peeled and deseeded
   pumpkin, finely sliced
salt
150ml/5fl oz/⅔ cup white wine vinegar
3 small shallots, finely sliced
2 small bay leaves
6 black peppercorns
a handful of basil leaves, plus extra
   to garnish

Preheat the oven to 180°C/350°F/gas mark 4. Lightly grease a baking sheet with olive oil, put the pumpkin slices on top, sprinkle with salt and drizzle with more olive oil. Roast in the oven for 30 minutes, until golden and cooked through but not mushy. Remove and leave to cool.

Put the vinegar, shallots, bay leaves and peppercorns in a small pan and bring to the boil. Remove from the heat and leave to cool.

In a non-metallic container, make layers of pumpkin, basil leaves and the vinegar marinade. Leave to marinate for at least 4 hours – or overnight in the fridge. Bring to room temperature before serving, drizzle over some extra virgin olive oil and scatter over a few fresh basil leaves.

# Sardine marinate all'arancia
## Sardines marinated in orange

Sardines are so good for you, and I am pleased to see they are now readily available on most supermarket fish counters ready cleaned and filleted and excellent value! Fish is often made in this way in Italy, known as *al carpione*; once cooked it is left to marinate and it was a popular way to preserve fish before the arrival of fridges. It makes an excellent antipasto served with a crunchy raw fennel salad.

Serves 4

1 egg
salt and freshly ground black pepper
70g/2½oz dried breadcrumbs
1 tbsp finely chopped parsley
4 sardines, 50–60g/about 2oz each,
    cleaned and filleted
plain (all-purpose) flour, to dust
vegetable oil for shallow frying

**for the marinade**
3 tbsp extra virgin olive oil
125g/4½oz shallots, finely chopped
2 tbsp white wine vinegar
grated zest and juice of 1 large orange

**for the fennel salad**
1 large fennel bulb, finely sliced
4 tbsp extra virgin olive oil

Put the egg in a bowl, season and beat well. Put the breadcrumbs on a plate and combine with the parsley. Dust the sardines in flour, shake off excess flour, dip into the egg mixture, then coat well with the breadcrumbs, gently pressing and flattening with the palms of your hands.

Heat some oil in a large frying pan. When hot, cook the sardines for a couple of minutes on each side until golden. Drain on kitchen paper and set aside.

For the marinade, put the olive oil in a small saucepan on a medium heat, add the shallots and cook until they have softened and are slightly golden. Stir in the vinegar and leave to infuse for a minute. Remove from the heat and leave to cool. Stir in the orange juice and zest. Pour over the sardines, cover with clingfilm (plastic wrap) and leave to marinate for at least 2 hours – or up to 3 days in the fridge; serve at room temperature.

For the fennel salad, put the sliced fennel in a bowl and mix well with olive oil, salt and pepper. Serve with the sardines.

# Insalata di coniglio alla Toscana
## Tuscan rabbit salad

I love the tangy taste that comes from cooking the rabbit in vinegar and wine; it is then marinated, resulting in tender, flavoursome pieces of meat. Served in a salad with bulgur wheat and beans, it makes a perfectly balanced, simple meal. If you prefer, you can substitute chicken for the rabbit.

To use dried borlotti beans, soak them in water overnight, then drain and simmer in fresh water for about 1 hour, or until the beans are tender (check the packet instructions). Drain and leave to cool.

Serves 4–6

700ml/1¼ pints/3 cups white
   wine vinegar
700ml/1¼ pints/3 cups dry white wine
½ tsp salt
1kg/2lb 4oz rabbit pieces on the bone
250g/9oz bulgur wheat
200g/7oz fresh or frozen broad
   (fava) beans
200g/7oz cooked or canned
   borlotti beans
1 small red onion, finely sliced
juice of 1 lemon

**for the marinade**
500ml/18fl oz/2 cups olive oil
3 garlic cloves, squashed and
   left whole
6 sage leaves
2 rosemary sprigs
1 red chilli, finely sliced

In a large saucepan, heat 700ml/1¼ pints/3 cups of water with the vinegar and wine. Add the salt and rabbit, bring to the boil, then reduce the heat and simmer for about 35 minutes, until the rabbit is tender and cooked through.

Combine the ingredients for the marinade and set aside.

Remove the rabbit from the pan and leave until cool enough to handle, then remove the flesh from the bones. Put the meat in the marinade, cover with clingfilm (plastic wrap) and leave to marinate for 2 hours.

Meanwhile, cook the bulgur wheat for about 15 minutes, until al dente – check the packet instructions. Drain and leave to cool. Cook the broad beans for about 10 minutes (less if using frozen beans), until tender but not mushy, drain and leave to cool.

Combine the cooked bulgur wheat, broad beans, borlotti beans and red onion, adding as much or as little of the olive oil from the marinade as you like, together with lemon juice to taste, and toss well. Place on a serving dish and top with the pieces of marinated rabbit.

# Insalata di manzo bollito
## Cold beef salad

This is a lovely light dish made from the boiled beef used to make beef broth (see page 25). The resulting meat is very tender and perfect served cold as a salad, with good bread.

Serves 4–6

1 quantity of beef from beef broth
  (see page 25)
1 bunch of spring onions
  (scallions),trimmed and
  roughly chopped
200g/7oz cherry tomatoes, halved
  or quartered, depending on size
20g/¾oz/2 tbsp black olives
salt and freshly ground black pepper
5 tbsp extra virgin olive oil
juice of 1 lemon
200g/7oz rocket (arugula)
40g/1½oz Parmesan shavings

Drain the beef from the broth, leave to cool, then chop into bite-size pieces and set aside.

Place the beef in a bowl together with the spring onions, tomatoes and olives and toss well with salt, pepper, olive oil and lemon juice. Add the rocket and stir in carefully. Divide among four or six plates and just before serving top with Parmesan shavings.

# Polpette di carne
## Meatballs

This is a fantastically simple recipe you can make with the beef cooked for the beef broth (see page 25); in the past, Italian housewives would always make *polpette* this way or with leftover roast beef. When we have leftover boiled or roast beef, my wife Liz often makes meatballs or burgers for the children. These meatballs can also be frozen. *Polpette* are delicious eaten as they are or with a tomato sauce, served with pasta or added to a lasagne. If you turn the beef into burgers, serve with some good bread buns, salad and cheese and enjoy, as my girls do, a homemade treat!

Makes about 40 meatballs or 20 burgers

1 quantity of beef from beef broth
  (see page 25)
3 tbsp extra virgin olive oil
2 onions, finely chopped
a handful of parsley, finely chopped
115g/4oz bread, grated into fine crumbs
100g/3½oz Parmesan, grated
salt and freshly ground black pepper
3 eggs
plain (all-purpose) flour, to dust
olive oil for frying

Drain the beef from the broth and chop into large chunks; put the chunks in a food processor and whizz until well minced (ground). Alternatively, chop the beef very finely with a sharp knife.

Heat the olive oil in a frying pan, add the onions and sweat on a low heat for about 10 minutes, until softened. Leave to cool.

Combine the minced beef with the cooled onion, parsley, breadcrumbs, Parmesan, salt and pepper to taste, and the eggs. Shape into balls about the size of walnuts; alternatively shape into burgers. Place on a lightly greased baking tin or dish, cover with clingfilm (plastic wrap) and place in the fridge for about an hour. Alternatively, place in a container, seal and freeze for later use.

Dust the meatballs with a little flour, heat some oil in a frying pan and fry the meatballs in the hot oil until lightly browned on all sides. Do this in batches, depending on the size of your pan. Drain on kitchen paper and keep warm until all are cooked. If you are making burgers, fry them for a couple of minutes on each side. Serve with pasta or buns and salad.

# Bollito misto con salsa verde

## Mixed boiled meats served with salsa verde

This typical Piemontese dish is usually made for special occasions involving large numbers of people. Traditionalists insist on seven prime cuts of beef and veal, seven lesser meats such as chicken, ox tongue and sausage, served with seven sauces, boiled vegetables and a bowl of the broth in which the meats were cooked. However, the recipe is adapted by different families to suit their needs. *Zampone* or *cotechino* sausage is usually included in *bollito misto* – you will find it in Italian delis. Here is my simplified version of this dish, with a tangy salsa verde (green sauce). You can also serve it with *mostarda di Cremona* (a traditional condiment of candied fruits in mustard, sold in Italian delis), horseradish sauce, mustard and pickled vegetables. The meats are simmered together in a large pan; the resulting broth is served as a starter with tortellini pasta (or kept as a stock for other dishes), and the meats are served as a main course.

Serves 10

500g/1lb 2oz ox tongue
500g/1lb 2oz piece of beef brisket
1 small chicken, weighing about
   1.2kg/2lb 10oz
1 large onion
2 celery stalks with leaves
2 carrots
4 cherry tomatoes
a handful of parsley, including stalks
salt
10 black peppercorns
6 potatoes, peeled and left whole
1 vacuum-packed zampone or
   cotechino sausage

**for the salsa verde**
2 large handfuls of parsley
50g/1¾oz baby gherkins (cornichons)
50g/1¾oz capers
1 garlic clove
4 anchovy fillets
40g/1½oz bread, soaked in a little
   lukewarm water
yolk from 1 hard-boiled egg
5 tbsp extra virgin olive oil

Wash the ox tongue under cold running water and pat dry with kitchen paper. Place in a large saucepan with cold water to cover, bring to the boil, skim off the scum, then reduce the heat, cover with a lid and cook gently for 1 hour, removing the scum from time to time.

Add the beef brisket and continue to simmer for 1 hour.

Add the chicken, onion, celery, carrots, tomatoes, parsley, salt and peppercorns and cook for 30 minutes. Add the potatoes and cook for another 30 minutes. At the same time, bring another saucepan of water to the boil, add the zampone or cotechino and cook according to the packet instructions.

To make the salsa verde: very finely chop the parsley, gherkins, capers, garlic, anchovies, bread and egg yolk – you can do this in a food processor, but I prefer the slight crunchiness you get by chopping with a knife. Put the chopped ingredients into a bowl and combine with the olive oil. This can be made 2–3 days ahead and stored in the fridge, but serve at room temperature.

When the meats are cooked, remove from the liquid and set aside. Leave the tongue to cool a little before peeling off the skin, then slice. Slice all the other meats and arrange on a large serving dish. Serve with the salsa verde (you can also serve the potatoes and vegetables).

# Insalata di pollo con giardiniera
## Chicken salad with preserved vegetables

This is a lovely dish made from the chicken cooked in the Chicken broth recipe (see page 26). Serve as an antipasto or a main course with lots of good bread to dip into the dressing. You will need to marinate it overnight in the fridge and you can leave the finished dish to infuse for another day. If you want a short cut, instead of preparing the vegetables, use a jar of ready-made preserved *giardiniera*, which is an Italian mixed vegetable pickle sold in good delis.

Serves 4

1 cooked chicken from chicken broth
   (see page 26)
a sprig of thyme, a couple of sage leaves
   and slices of red chilli, to garnish
   (optional)

**for the marinade**
300ml/10fl oz/1¼ cups olive oil
3 garlic cloves, left whole
1 red chilli, sliced
4 sprigs of thyme
2 sprigs of rosemary
4 sage leaves

**for the vegetables**
200ml/7fl oz/scant 1 cup red
   wine vinegar
salt
100g/3½oz green beans, topped
   and tailed
2 celery stalks, sliced
2 small carrots, finely sliced
10 baby onions, peeled and left whole
100g/3½oz celeriac (celery root),
   peeled and cut into bite-size chunks
¼ red pepper, cut into chunks
   (optional)
a few cauliflower florets (optional)

Remove the chicken from the broth and leave to cool. Remove the skin and bones and break the flesh into pieces. Place in a dish and set aside.

Put all the marinade ingredients into a saucepan and heat gently, but do not bring to the boil. Remove from the heat and pour over the chicken, cover with clingfilm (plastic wrap) and leave in the fridge overnight.

Remove the chicken from the fridge and leave at room temperature for about 20 minutes.

Meanwhile, to cook the vegetables, put 400ml/14fl oz/1⅔ cups water in a saucepan with the vinegar and a couple of good pinches of salt, bring to the boil, add the vegetables and blanch for 5 minutes. Drain and leave to cool.

Add the vegetables to the chicken mixture and toss well. Garnish with herbs and chilli if desired. Serve immediately or leave in the fridge to infuse for up to 24 hours, but serve at room temperature.

# Liatina e' puorc

## Pork in aspic jelly

Gelatine or aspic jelly was used in ancient Rome as a stiffening agent in the kitchen; in medieval times meat and fish gelatines were served at grand banquets. Gelatine, these days, is mostly used by producers of marshmallows and gummy sweets and is sold in thin leaves for home use when making jellies or panna cotta. But it is derived from the feet (and other parts) of pigs and calves. Until relatively recently in rural areas of Italy, nothing was wasted when a pig was killed, and parts like the trotter, ear, tail and even snout were used in dishes like this. We used to eat this dish when I was a boy in Italy; that's why I have kept the title in Neapolitan dialect. Jellied pork is still popular in the Campania region and Sicily. It is very simple to prepare and most butchers will be happy to sell you the pig's parts for a minimal cost.

Serves 10–12

1 pig's trotter
1 pig's ear
1 pig's tail
1kg/2lb 4oz mixed pork meat, such as chops, stewing chunks, neck
10 bay leaves, plus a few extra to garnish
1 tbsp salt
3 tbsp white wine vinegar
juice of ½ lemon
freshly ground black pepper
30g/1oz pine kernels
30g/1oz sultanas (golden raisins)

First clean the pig's trotter, ear and tail under cold running water, scrubbing well and ensuring all hairs and impurities are removed. Put the pieces in a large saucepan with the pork meat, 10 bay leaves and the salt and cover with cold water. Bring to the boil, skim off the scum, then reduce the heat, partially cover with a lid and gently simmer for 2¾ hours, removing any scum from time to time.

Add the vinegar and simmer for a further 15 minutes. Remove the pork meat and leave to cool. Discard the trotter, ear and tail. Strain the liquid through a fine sieve, add the lemon juice and set aside.

Using your fingers, tear the cooled meat into pieces, discarding any fat. Put the pieces of meat in a large terrine, sprinkle with some black pepper, half the pine kernels and sultanas and three or four bay leaves. Pour over the liquid and leave in a cool place to set for about an hour, then scatter over the remaining pine kernels, sultanas and a couple more bay leaves. Cover with clingfilm (plastic wrap) and leave in a cool place overnight to set completely. If you are making this on a warm day, place in the fridge once set, otherwise leave at room temperature.

# Sgombro marinato alla menta

## Marinated mackerel with mint

A really easy dish using one of my favourite fish, mackerel. It makes a delicious antipasto or light lunch, served with lots of good bread to mop up the oil. It's not a dish you can hurry: the fish is first steam-cooked in parchment paper and then marinated, first in vinegar and then in olive oil. The longer you leave it in the oil, the more the flavour improves: it can be kept, covered, in the fridge for up to a week.

Serves 4

800g/1lb 12oz mackerel fillets
salt
400ml/14fl oz/1⅔ cups white
  wine vinegar
1 garlic clove, finely sliced
a handful of mint leaves
abundant olive oil, to marinate

Take a large sheet of baking parchment and wrap each fillet separately, tying them with kitchen string into a parcel – this is to prevent them from breaking during cooking. Place in a pan of salted water, bring to the boil, reduce the heat and simmer for 3 minutes. Alternatively, cook the fillets in a steamer.

Remove, drain the parcels and open carefully. Put the fillets in a non-metallic container or dish, pour over the vinegar, cover with clingfilm (plastic wrap) and leave in the fridge to marinate for at least 4 hours.

Carefully remove the mackerel and place in a clean container together with the garlic and mint leaves, and cover with olive oil. Cover with clingfilm (plastic wrap) and leave in the fridge overnight.

Remove from the fridge and bring to room temperature before eating. Serve with lots of good bread.

# Insalata di polipo

## Octopus salad

This is one of my favourite meals. It's made from the octopus cooked in the octopus broth recipe (see page 29). The flesh is cut into pieces and simply tossed in extra virgin olive oil and lemon juice. It can be made the day before and kept, covered, in the fridge – but get it out 30 minutes before you want to eat, as it is best served at room temperature.

Serves 4–6

1 cooked octopus from octopus broth
   (see page 29)
8 tbsp extra virgin olive oil
juice of 1 large lemon
a good pinch of salt
2 garlic cloves, finely sliced
bunch of parsley, roughly chopped
1 small red chilli
12 large green olives, sliced in half

Take the drained octopus and set aside about 100ml/3½fl oz/scant ½ cup of the broth and leave to cool.

Put the octopus on a chopping board and chop into bite-size pieces – you can use scissors to cut the tentacles. Place the pieces in a large bowl. Add the rest of the ingredients, including the reserved broth, mix well, and leave to rest for at least 30 minutes. Serve with lots of good bread.

# Carciofi ripieni

## Filled artichokes

Artichokes are very popular in Italy, especially in the south, where they grow in abundance. The season begins in spring and they are often eaten at Easter time. I love artichokes; they are light and digestible and can be cooked in so many different ways. In this slow-cooked stove-top dish they are filled with a tasty mixture of pancetta and vegetables.

Serves 4

4 globe artichokes
juice of 1 lemon
1–2 small carrots, scrubbed and halved
1 celery stalk with leaves
1 small onion, halved
1 potato, scrubbed
2 cherry tomatoes
a pinch of salt

**for the filling**
4 tbsp extra virgin olive oil, plus
   extra to drizzle
40g/1½oz pancetta, cubed
2 shallots, finely sliced
1 garlic clove, chopped
1 small courgette (zucchini),
   finely diced
½ aubergine (eggplant), finely diced
a handful of parsley, roughly chopped
15g/½oz/2 tbsp pine nuts
40g/1½oz Parmesan, grated
freshly ground black pepper
a small bunch of basil leaves (optional)

First clean and prepare the artichokes: using a sharp knife, remove the bottom outer leaves and cut off the stalks. Trim the base so the bottom is flat and the artichoke can stand upright. With your fingers, gently open out the artichoke leaves until you can see the hairy choke. With a small teaspoon, remove and discard the choke, which is inedible. Place the artichokes in a bowl of water with the lemon juice in order to prevent discoloration while you prepare the filling.

To make the filling, heat the olive oil in a saucepan, add the pancetta and fry until crisp, remove and set aside. Add the shallots and garlic to the pan and sweat until softened, ensuring you don't burn the garlic; remove and set aside. In the same pan, stir-fry the courgette and aubergine for 8–10 minutes, until soft but not mushy. Remove from the heat and combine with the pancetta, shallots, parsley, pine nuts, Parmesan and pepper.

*Continues overleaf*

Remove the artichokes from the water and turn them upside down to drain. Open them up and fill the cavity with the pancetta mixture; tie with string to ensure the filling does not fall out and, if you like, tuck a few basil leaves into the top of each artichoke. Place in a pan large enough to hold all four artichokes snugly.

Add the carrots, celery, onion, potato and tomatoes. Sprinkle the artichokes with a little salt, drizzle with olive oil and fill the pan with water to come halfway up the artichokes. Put the pan on a medium–high heat and bring to the boil, then immediately reduce the heat to low, cover with a lid and simmer gently for 1¼ hours. Lift the artichokes out of the pan using a slotted spoon and serve one per person, with a little of the broth. And don't forget to eat the potato and carrot!

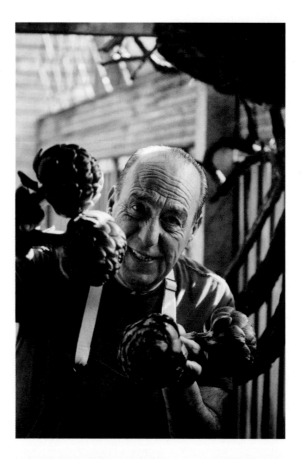

# STEWS

Stews are popular all over the world; they are warming, welcoming, and a wonderful way to use economical cuts of meat. Pieces of meat that are slowly cooked in a sauce with herbs, spices and seasonings are often far more tender and tasty than a quickly grilled steak, and with the inclusion of vegetables can be a meal in themselves – or serve with polenta (cornmeal), rice, mashed potatoes or lots of good bread to mop up the juices.

The classic Italian way of preparing a stew begins with a *soffritto*, a gently fried mix of onion, celery and carrot – this important step forms the base of the stew, ensuring maximum flavour. The sealing or browning of the pieces of meat is equally important, giving a rich flavour and adding colour to the stew. It is important to cook the stew on a very gentle heat because boiling will toughen the meat. To enhance the flavour, stews are best made the day before and gently reheated when required.

You can usually find ready-cut chunks of meat clearly marked 'for stewing' in supermarkets, or your butcher will cut the meat for you. If you are beginning with a larger piece of meat, it should be cut into cubes of roughly 4–5cm/1½– 2 inches; pieces that are too small will fall apart and may dry out during cooking.

The following are ideal cuts for stewing:

Lamb: scrag end and middle neck, shoulder, knuckle/shank

Beef: neck, chuck, blade, brisket, thick flank, thin flank, skirt, shin/shank, topside, silverside, knuckle

Pork: shoulder – although you can use any cut, shoulder is the most economical

Italian stews are as varied as the country: from a rich Tyrolean goulash originating in the Austrian-influenced Alpine region of Trentino-Alto Adige, to my slow-cooked vegetable stew using the typical sun-drenched ingredients of the southern regions – you will find a dish to satisfy every taste and mood.

# Goulash Tirolese

## Tyrolean beef stew

This classic stew from the Trentino-Alto Adige or South Tyrol region of northern Italy is slow cooked with onions, cumin and paprika – its distinct central European flavour is influenced by neighbouring Austria. The gradual addition of stock gives this stew a gentle flavour; pancetta is added, so be careful not to make your stock too salty. This dish is traditionally served with runny polenta (cornmeal). It is also delicious with a piece of good country bread whose soft part is removed, cubed and toasted; the goulash is served in the bread crust and the toasted bits sprinkled on top – a dish fit for an Austrian king!

Serves 4

3 tbsp extra virgin olive oil
2 large onions, sliced
100g/3½oz pancetta, cubed
about 1 litre/1¾ pints/4 cups hot
    vegetable stock (see page 36)
    – or use a stock cube
1kg/2lb 4oz stewing beef, cut
    into chunks
2 garlic cloves, sliced
1 tsp cumin seeds, crushed
1 tsp paprika
2 sprigs of thyme
polenta (cornmeal) or toasted
    country bread, to serve

### For a slow cooker

Cook the onions, pancetta and beef as above. Once the beef is browned add 750ml/1¼ pints/3 cups stock, the garlic, cumin, paprika, thyme and pancetta. Bring to the boil, stirring, then transfer to a large slow cooker pot, press the meat beneath the liquid, cover and cook on Low for 8–9 hours.

Heat the olive oil in a large saucepan and sweat the onions on a medium heat for about 5 minutes, stirring all the time to prevent sticking, until softened. Remove and set aside.

Add the pancetta to the pan and cook on a medium heat until coloured but not burnt. Remove from the pan and set aside. Return the onions to the pan, add about 3 tablespoons of stock and cook for a minute or so until the liquid has evaporated.

Add the beef, increase the heat and brown the meat all over. Add 100ml/3½fl oz/scant ½ cup of stock, reduce the heat to low, cover with a lid and cook very gently for 30 minutes, then add another 100ml/3½fl oz/scant ½ cup of stock and continue to cook for 30 minutes.

Stir in the garlic, cumin, paprika, thyme and pancetta. Add 400ml/14fl oz/1⅔ cups of stock, cover with a lid and cook on a low heat for a further 1 hour, gradually adding more stock and stirring from time to time to ensure the meat doesn't stick.

Remove from the heat and serve with toasted country bread or runny polenta.

# Stufato di manzo al cioccolato

## Slow-cooked marinated beef with chocolate

Although adding chocolate to savoury dishes is a South American tradition, it has become increasingly popular in Italian dishes – cocoa powder is even added to pasta dough! I must say I am not too keen on these gimmicky recipes; however, the addition of a little good-quality dark chocolate to slow-cooked beef does enrich the sauce.

Serves 4

1kg/2lb 4oz stewing beef, cut
   into chunks
2 onions, sliced
2 carrots, sliced
3 bay leaves
1 garlic clove, left whole, crushed
250ml/9fl oz/1 cup red wine
2 tsp red wine vinegar
3 tbsp extra virgin olive oil
a handful of parsley, finely chopped
2 sprigs of thyme, finely chopped
400ml/14fl oz/1⅔ cups beef stock
   (see page 25) – or use a stock cube
30g/1oz dark chocolate, grated
salt and freshly ground black pepper
3 potatoes, cut into chunks

Rinse the beef under cold running water and pat dry. Place in a bowl with the onions, carrots, bay leaves and garlic. Pour in the wine and vinegar, cover with clingfilm (plastic wrap) and put in the fridge to marinate for 8 hours or overnight.

Discard the garlic clove, drain the liquid and set aside. Heat the olive oil in a large saucepan and brown the beef well all over. Add the onions, carrots and bay leaves and sweat for about 4 minutes, until the onion has softened. Stir in the parsley and thyme, pour in the marinade liquid and stock and stir in the chocolate, some salt and pepper. Reduce the heat, partially cover with a lid and cook on a low heat for 1½ hours.

Remove the lid, add the potatoes and cook on a medium heat for a further 30 minutes, until the potatoes are cooked and the liquid has reduced slightly. Serve immediately.

---

### For a slow cooker

Marinate the beef as above. Brown the beef, then add the vegetables, herbs, marinade liquid and 300ml10fl oz/1¼ cups beef stock, then the chocolate and salt and pepper. Bring to the boil, stirring, then transfer to a large slow cooker pot, press the meat beneath the liquid, cover and cook on Low for 8–9 hours.

Cook the potatoes in a saucepan of boiling water for 15 minutes until just tender. Drain and stir into the slow cooker pot. Cover and cook on Low for 30 minutes. Stir before serving.

# Spezzatino casalingo

## Everyday beef and vegetable stew

This is the family stew my wife Liz normally makes at home – nothing fancy or complicated, just good old-fashioned comfort food. It is delicious, nutritious and good value for money, using economical pieces of stewing beef and root vegetables. If you don't have red wine to hand or don't want to open a new bottle, simply replace with more stock. Serve with mashed potatoes for a satisfying meal.

Serves 4

800g/1lb 12oz stewing beef, cut
   into chunks
salt and freshly ground black pepper
plain (all-purpose) flour, to dust
5 tbsp extra virgin olive oil
2 onions, finely sliced
2 large carrots, cut into chunks
2 parsnips, cut into chunks
2 sprigs of thyme
50ml/2fl oz/3 tbsp red wine
400ml/14fl oz/1⅔ cups beef stock
   (see page 25) – or use a stock cube
2 tsp tomato purée (paste)

Rub salt and pepper all over the chunks of beef and dust lightly with flour. Heat 2 tablespoons of the olive oil in a large saucepan, add the beef and brown well all over on a high heat. Remove the meat and set aside.

In the same pan, heat the remaining olive oil and sweat the onions on a medium heat for a couple of minutes. Add the carrots, parsnips and thyme and sweat for another 2 minutes.

Return the meat to the pan, increase the heat to high, add the wine and allow to evaporate. Add the stock and tomato purée, reduce the heat to low, cover with a lid and cook gently for 1 hour 45 minutes, stirring from time to time.

Remove from the heat and serve immediately with mashed potatoes or with some good crusty bread.

**For a slow cooker**

Dust the beef with flour and brown as above. Using a slotted spoon, transfer to a large slow cooker pot. Sweat the vegetables as above, add the wine and evaporate. Add the stock and tomato purée, bring to the boil, stirring, then pour over the meat and press the meat and vegetables beneath the liquid. Cover and cook on Low for 8–9 hours. Stir before serving.

# Ossobuco alla Milanese in bianco
## Braised veal shins

There are two ways of making this classic Milanese dish – with or without tomatoes. The latter, known in Italian as *in bianco*, is actually the original version: the veal is slowly braised with vegetables, white wine and stock and garnished with gremolada for extra flavour and colour. Veal shin or knuckle is a cheap, tough cut but extremely flavoursome and ideal for slow cooking. The name *ossobuco* in Italian means 'bone with a hole', a reference to the hollow marrow bone at the centre of the cross-cut veal shin. Ask your butcher for veal shin for ossobuco and he will cut the pieces for you for this excellent dish. In Milan, this is traditionally served with risotto alla Milanese – saffron risotto.

Serves 4

4 cross-cut slices of veal shin,
   about 300g/10½oz each
plain (all-purpose) flour, to dust
50g/1¾oz/4 tbsp butter
3 tbsp extra virgin olive oil
1 onion, finely chopped
1 carrot, finely chopped
150ml/5fl oz/⅔ cup dry white wine
salt and freshly ground black pepper
500ml/18fl oz/2 cups veal or chicken
   stock (see page 26) – or use a
   stock cube

**for the gremolada**
1 garlic clove, finely chopped
a handful of parsley, finely chopped
grated zest of ½ lemon

Using kitchen scissors, slightly snip the skin around the veal shins (this is done to prevent the meat from curling up during cooking). Dust the meat with flour, shake off any excess and set aside.

Heat the butter and oil in a large saucepan, add the onion and carrot and gently sweat until softened. Increase the heat to medium, add the veal shins and brown on both sides. Add the wine and allow to evaporate. Season with salt and pepper, add the stock, reduce the heat, partially cover with a lid and cook on a low heat for 1½ hours, or until the meat is tender.

Meanwhile, prepare the gremolada by combining all the ingredients together.

When the veal is cooked, remove from the heat and leave to rest for 5 minutes. Sprinkle with the gremolada and serve.

---

**For a slow cooker**

Sweat the vegetables and brown the meat as above, add the wine and evaporate. Add the salt, pepper and stock, bring to the boil, then transfer to a large slow cooker pot, make sure the veal is beneath the stock, then cover and cook on Low for 6–7 hours. Serve as above.

# Spezzatino di maiale

## Pork stew

A homey stew that is a complete meal in itself. The addition of pancetta or bacon enhances the flavour of the pork. It can be made the day before and reheated when required, adding the peas after you have reheated the stew. Serve with good bread to mop up the sauce.

Serves 4

650g/1lb 7oz stewing pork, cut
   into chunks
salt and freshly ground black pepper
plain (all-purpose) flour, to dust
3 tbsp extra virgin olive oil
1 onion, finely chopped
1 celery stalk, finely sliced
2 carrots, halved lengthways and
   cut into chunks
3 fresh sage leaves
50g/1¾oz pancetta slices or streaky
   bacon, roughly chopped
75ml/2½fl oz/5 tbsp dry white wine
250ml/9fl oz/1 cup vegetable stock
   (see page 36) – or use a stock cube
400g/14oz potatoes, cut into chunks
150g/5½oz/generous 1 cup frozen peas

Season the pork with salt and pepper and dust with flour, shake off any excess flour and set aside.

Heat the olive oil in a large saucepan. Add the onion, celery, carrots, sage and pancetta and sweat on a medium heat. Add the pork and brown well all over.

Add the wine and allow to evaporate. Add 100ml/3½fl oz/ scant ½ cup stock, reduce the heat to low, cover with a lid and cook for 30 minutes.

Add the remaining stock. After 15 minutes, add the potatoes and cook for another hour.

Five minutes before the end of cooking time, add the peas. Remove from the heat and serve.

---

**For a slow cooker**

Heat the oil in a large deep frying pan and sweat the vegetables and pancetta as above. Add the floured pork and brown, then add the wine and evaporate. Pour in 250ml/9fl oz/1 cup stock and bring to the boil, stirring. Cut the potatoes into 2.5cm/1 inch chunks (these can take longer to cook than meat so don't make any bigger) and place in a large slow cooker pot, pour over the hot pork mixture and press the meat and potatoes beneath the liquid. Cover and cook on Low for 8–9 hours. Stir in the frozen peas, with a little extra hot stock, if needed. Cover and cook on Low for 20 minutes.

# Cassoeula

## Braised pork and cabbage

This dish from the Lombardy region of northern Italy was traditionally made on the feast of Saint Anthony on 17 January to mark the end of the pig slaughtering season. No part of the pig was ever wasted and the cheaper cuts, such as trotters, skin, ears, nose, ribs and tail, were used to make this stew – the better parts were for curing into hams and salami. This dish is still popular today and I have adapted it with more readily available cuts of pork. Serve with runny polenta (cornmeal), as they do in Lombardy, or mashed potatoes for a perfect winter warmer. The addition of Parmesan rind gives the stew an extra bit of flavour. When you finish a piece of Parmesan, don't discard the rind; wrap it in clingfilm (plastic wrap) and store in the fridge to add to soups and stews.

Serves 4

1 onion, finely chopped
4 carrots, roughly chopped
2 celery stalks, roughly chopped
4 pork ribs, about 100g/3½oz each
225g/8oz pork loin steaks, cut into strips
200g/7oz pork sausages
50g/1¾oz salami, cubed
800ml/28fl oz/3½ cups vegetable
    stock(see page 36) – or use
    a stock cube
200g/7oz tomato passata
    (strained tomatoes)
1kg/2lb 4oz savoy cabbage,
    roughly chopped
a few pieces of Parmesan rind (optional)
salt and freshly ground black pepper

Heat 100ml/3½fl oz/scant ½ cup water in a large saucepan, add the onion, carrots and celery, cover with a lid and steam-fry on a medium heat for 4 minutes.

Add the ribs, loin, sausages and salami. Combine the stock and passata and add to the saucepan. Add the cabbage and the Parmesan rind, if using, some salt and pepper, cover with a lid and cook on a gentle heat for 2 hours. Remove from the heat, season with salt and pepper to taste and serve.

---

### For a slow cooker

Steam-fry the onion, carrots and celery as above. Add the ribs, loin, sausages and salami. Mix the stock with the passata and add to the meat with the Parmesan rind, salt and pepper. Bring to the boil then transfer to a large slow cooker pot. Cover and cook on Low for 7 hours. Add the cabbage, ladle over some of the hot liquid, then cover and cook on Low for 1–1¼ hours until the cabbage is very tender. Stir before serving.

# Montone alla contadina
## Rustic mutton stew

I love mutton. As a boy, I remember, during the winter months, farmers would bring mutton to the village to sell and my father would always buy some to be slow-cooked with lots of herbs in a casserole. Mutton cut into chunks for stewing is now available from supermarkets; not only is it more economical than lamb, I find it more flavoursome, especially when making stews. It is ideal for slow-cooking and with the addition of potatoes is a complete one-pot meal.

Serves 4

4 tbsp extra virgin olive oil
1 large onion, finely sliced
2 garlic cloves, finely sliced
1kg/2lb 4oz mutton pieces
200ml/7fl oz/scant 1 cup red wine
2 bay leaves
4 sage leaves
2 sprigs of rosemary
salt and freshly ground black pepper
1 litre/1¾ pints/4 cups vegetable stock
  (see page 36) – or use a stock cube
1 tbsp tomato purée (paste)
600g/1lb 5oz potatoes, peeled and
  cut into chunks

Heat the olive oil in a large saucepan, add the onion and garlic and sweat for a couple of minutes. Add the mutton and brown well all over. Reduce the heat, add the wine, and allow to evaporate gradually on a low heat for about 15 minutes.

Stir in the herbs, some salt and pepper and 600ml/20fl oz/2½ cups of stock and cook on a low heat, partially covered with a lid, for 2 hours.

Add the remaining stock with the tomato purée and potatoes and cook for a further 25 minutes, until the potatoes are cooked. Remove from the heat, season with salt and pepper to taste and serve.

---

### For a slow cooker

Sweat the onion and garlic, brown the meat and evaporate the wine as above. Add the herbs, salt and pepper and tomato purée, then add 750ml/1¼ pints/3 cups stock and bring to the boil. Cut the potatoes into 2.5cm/1 inch chunks and place in a large slow cooker pot, add the meat and onion, then pour in the liquid. Press the meat and potatoes beneath the liquid, cover and cook on Low for 8–10 hours. Serve as above.

# Agnello con i fagioli

## Lamb stew with beans

This rustic lamb stew is a perfect winter warmer and a complete meal in one pot. I really like to use dried beans, which need to be soaked overnight and cooked before being added to the stew. However, to save time, you could use canned beans and add them towards the end of the cooking time.

Serves 4

150g/5½oz/¾ cup dried white kidney
   beans or cannellini beans, soaked
   in water overnight
3 tbsp extra virgin olive oil
1 onion, finely chopped
375g/13oz shoulder of lamb, cut
   into chunks
40g/1½oz pancetta, diced
1 carrot, diced
1 clove
1 bay leaf
100ml/3½fl oz/scant ½ cup dry
   white wine
3 tbsp canned chopped tomato
300ml/10fl oz/1¼ cups vegetable stock
   (see page 36) – or use a stock cube

**to serve**
country bread, toasted and drizzled
   with extra virgin olive oil

Drain the beans and put them in a large saucepan with plenty of cold water, bring to the boil, then reduce the heat, partially cover with a lid and simmer for 1½ hours, or until tender but not mushy. Drain the beans and set aside.

Meanwhile, heat the olive oil in a large saucepan, add the onion and sweat for about 3 minutes until softened. Add the lamb and brown all over. Add the pancetta, carrot, clove and bay leaf and stir-fry on a medium heat for 5 minutes. Pour in the wine and allow to evaporate. Add the tomato and cook for 3 minutes, then add the stock. Reduce the heat, cover with a lid and cook on a low heat for 2 hours.

Add the beans and cook for a further 15 minutes. Serve with slices of toasted country bread.

---

### For a slow cooker

Heat the oil in a large deep frying pan, sweat the onion and brown the lamb as above. Add the pancetta, carrot, clove and bay leaf, then the wine, and evaporate as above. Add the tomato and 300ml/ 10fl oz/1¼ cups stock. Bring to the boil, stirring, then transfer to a large or medium slow cooker pot, press the meat beneath the liquid, cover and cook on Low for 7–8 hours.

Drain 2 x 380g/13oz cartons cannellini beans (or use about 500g/ 1lb 2oz cooked dried beans), stir into the slow cooker pot with a little extra hot stock, if needed. Cover and cook on Low for 30 minutes. Stir before serving.

# Spezzatino d'agnello con zucca e zafferano

## Lamb stew with butternut squash and saffron

This hearty lamb stew with butternut squash and potato is full of colour – orange from the squash, yellow from saffron and a hint of red from tomato and chilli. Simple to prepare, this one-pot meal makes a delicious family meal or an informal dinner with friends.

Serves 4

700g/1lb 9oz stewing lamb, cut
 into chunks
salt and freshly ground black pepper
3 tbsp extra virgin olive oil
1 onion, finely chopped
2 garlic cloves, finely chopped
1 red chilli, halved lengthways
2 sprigs of rosemary
4 small sage leaves
a pinch of saffron, diluted in
 1 tbsp water
2 tbsp canned chopped tomatoes
4 tbsp dry white wine
200ml/7fl oz/scant 1 cup vegetable stock
 (see page 36) – or use a stock cube
200g/7oz potato, cut into large chunks
400g/14oz butternut squash, peeled
 and cut into large chunks

Rub the lamb all over with salt and pepper. Heat the olive oil in a large saucepan, add the meat and brown on all sides, then remove and set aside.

Add the onion, garlic and chilli to the pan and sweat for a couple of minutes. Return the lamb to the pan, then add the herbs, saffron and tomato. Add the wine and allow to evaporate. Add the stock, cover with a lid and cook on a very slow heat for 1 hour.

Add the potato and butternut squash and continue to cook for 30 minutes. Remove from the heat and leave to rest for a couple of minutes before serving.

---

### For a slow cooker

Brown the meat, sweat the vegetables and add the herbs, saffron and tomato as above; add the wine and allow to evaporate. Add 350ml/12fl oz/1½ cups stock and bring to the boil, stirring. Cut the potato and squash into 2.5cm/1 inch chunks. Put the potatoes into a large slow cooker pot, pour over the lamb mixture, press the lamb beneath the liquid and scatter the pumpkin on top. Cover and cook on Low for 8–9 hours. Stir before serving.

# Coniglio marinato all'agrodolce

## Sweet and sour marinated rabbit

I love rabbit and can't understand why it is not more widely available. The meat is tender, light and very digestible; in Italy, rabbit is given to weaning babies, convalescents and the elderly. You can order rabbit from good butchers, or if, like me, you shoot, the countryside is full of them. I often marinate rabbit because it rids the meat of that slightly gamey taste it can have; it can be marinated the day before and left in the fridge overnight. Once cooked, the rabbit is finished with a tangy sweet and sour sauce, giving the meat a real kick. Delicious served with slices of toasted country bread. If you prefer, chicken can be substituted for the rabbit.

Serves 4

1kg/2lb 4oz rabbit pieces on the bone, cleaned with a damp cloth
plain (all-purpose) flour, to dust
5 tbsp extra virgin olive oil
1 small onion, finely chopped
salt and freshly ground black pepper
5 tbsp vegetable stock

**for the marinade**
1 small onion, finely sliced
175ml/6fl oz/¾ cup red wine
a handful of parsley, finely chopped
2 bay leaves
8 black peppercorns
1 garlic clove, left whole
1 tsp thyme leaves
salt

**for the agrodolce**
20g/¾oz/1½ tbsp caster (superfine) sugar
a knob of butter
4 tbsp red wine vinegar
30g/1oz/3 tbsp sultanas (golden raisins), soaked in lukewarm water for about 20 minutes, then drained
15g/½oz/2 tbsp pine nuts

Put all the marinade ingredients in a small saucepan and bring to the boil, then remove from the heat and leave to cool. Put the rabbit in a dish, pour over the marinade, cover with clingfilm (plastic wrap) and leave in the fridge for at least 2 hours.

Remove the rabbit from the marinade, pat dry and dust with flour.

Heat the olive oil in a large frying pan, add the onion and sweat for a minute, then add the rabbit and brown all over. Pour over the marinade and cook on a low heat, uncovered, for about 15 minutes until the liquid has evaporated. Add salt, pepper and stock, cover with a lid and cook for 25 minutes on a medium–low heat until the rabbit is cooked through and the sauce has reduced.

Meanwhile, for the agrodolce, put the sugar and 2 tablespoons water in a small saucepan on a medium heat and stir until the sugar has dissolved. Stir in the butter until melted, then the vinegar and sultanas and bring to the boil for a minute. Pour this over the cooked rabbit, mixing it with the sauce, sprinkle with the pine nuts and serve.

# Scottiglia di capriolo
## Venison casserole

Scottiglia is a slow-cooked Tuscan stew or casserole that is usually made with whatever the hunter has managed to catch, so you could substitute wild boar, rabbit or hare for the venison in this recipe. Many supermarkets now sell farmed venison; 'casserole venison' is cut up ready for stewing. The meat is first marinated overnight for maximum tenderness and flavour and then slow-cooked for a rich-tasting casserole. Delicious served with runny polenta (cornmeal).

Serves 4

1kg/2lb 4oz venison haunch or
   casserole venison, cut into
   4–5 cm/ 1½–2-inch chunks
plain (all-purpose) flour, to dust
6 tbsp extra virgin olive oil
2 sprigs of rosemary
3 sage leaves
2 bay leaves
1 onion, sliced
2 garlic cloves, crushed
1 celery stalk, chopped
2 carrots, roughly chopped
salt and freshly ground black pepper
300ml/10fl oz/1¼ cups beef stock
   (see page 25) – or use a stock cube

**for the marinade**
75ml/2½fl oz/5 tbsp red wine vinegar
250ml/9fl oz/1 cup red wine
15 juniper berries
15 black peppercorns
3 bay leaves

Put the venison in a bowl. Combine all the marinade ingredients and pour over the meat, cover with clingfilm (plastic wrap) and leave in the fridge overnight.

Remove the venison from the marinade, reserving the liquid, and pat the meat dry. Dust the meat with flour and shake off any excess.

Heat the olive oil in a large saucepan on a high heat, add the meat and brown well all over. Reduce the heat, add the herbs, onion, garlic, celery, carrots and sweat for a couple of minutes. Season with salt and pepper. Add the marinade and cook on a high heat for a couple of minutes. Add the stock, reduce the heat to low, cover with a lid and cook for 2½ hours, until the meat is tender. Serve with runny polenta.

---

**For a slow cooker**

Marinate the venison as above. Drain, dust with flour and brown the meat, then transfer to a large slow cooker pot. Sweat the herbs, vegetables and garlic, season, then add the marinade and stock. Bring to the boil, pour over the venison, cover and cook on Low for 8–9 hours. Stir before serving.

# Pollo alla cacciatora

## Hunter's chicken

This classic Italian dish is renowned all over the world and often seen on the menus of Italian restaurants. The title *alla cacciatora* ('in the style of the hunter') suggests it was probably first made with game birds or rabbit. However, as with many Italian dishes, it also has roots in the *cucina povera*, when people used whatever meagre ingredients they had to hand; in this case, a chicken or, more likely, an old hen, was slaughtered for a special occasion and, to make it go further, enriched with whatever vegetables and herbs were available in the garden as well as a splash of homemade wine. It is made all over Italy and here I have recreated it in the way it is normally made in my region of Campania, using lots of herbs and fresh tomatoes. I like to serve this rustic dish with slices of toasted country bread drizzled with extra virgin olive oil.

Serves 4

750g/1lb 10oz chicken thighs
    and drumsticks
salt and freshly ground black pepper
3 tbsp extra virgin olive oil
1 large onion, finely sliced
1 garlic clove, crushed and left whole
1 small red chilli, sliced
2 sprigs of rosemary
2 sprigs of thyme
a handful of parsley, roughly chopped
2 bay leaves
4 sage leaves
125ml/4fl oz/½ cup dry white wine
1½ tbsp tomato purée (paste),
    dissolved in 3 tbsp lukewarm water
175g/6oz cherry tomatoes, halved

Rub the chicken pieces all over with salt and pepper. Heat the olive oil in a large saucepan, add the chicken and seal well all over.

Add the onion, garlic, chilli and herbs and cook for a couple of minutes on a medium heat. Add the wine, increase the heat and allow the wine to evaporate slightly. Add the diluted tomato purée, then stir in the cherry tomatoes. Reduce the heat to low, cover with a lid and cook gently for 1¼ hours, until the chicken is cooked through; the flesh should come away from the bone and there should be no sign of pink when you pierce the thickest part. Serve hot.

### For a slow cooker

Heat the oil in a large deep frying pan and cook the chicken as above. Continue as above, add the tomatoes, plus 300ml/10fl oz/1¼ cups chicken stock. Bring to the boil, then transfer to a large slow cooker pot. Cover and cook on Low for 7–8 hours or until there are no pink juices when the chicken is pierced with a small knife.

# Verdure estive stufate
## Summer vegetable stew

This simple but very tasty vegetable stew puts the flavours and colours of the Mediterranean on a plate. The slow, gentle cooking brings all the flavours of the vegetables and other ingredients together. I like to make this with lots of chilli and serve with couscous for a light but nutritious meal. It can be made in advance and in summer can be eaten cold if desired. Although it uses what I consider to be summer vegetables, it can be made at any time of the year.

Serves 4

4 tbsp extra virgin olive oil
2 red onions, finely sliced
2 celery stalks with leaves, sliced
3 garlic cloves, sliced
1 red chilli, finely chopped
5 anchovy fillets
1 tbsp capers
140g/5oz/¾ cup green olives
1 red (bell) pepper, cut into thick slices
1 yellow (bell) pepper, thickly sliced
1 aubergine (eggplant), cut into chunks
2 courgettes (zucchini), cut into chunks
200g/7oz green beans, sliced in half
3 tbsp dry white wine
300g/10½oz cherry tomatoes, halved
a handful of basil leaves
salt

Heat the olive oil in a large saucepan, add the onions, celery, garlic and chilli and sweat on a medium heat for a couple of minutes. Add the anchovy fillets and stir with a wooden spoon until dissolved. Add the capers and olives. Stir in the peppers, aubergine, courgettes and beans. Add the wine and allow to evaporate. Add the tomatoes, basil leaves and a pinch of salt. Reduce the heat, cover with a lid and cook gently for 1 hour. Serve with couscous.

**For a slow cooker**

Follow the recipe above and once all the ingredients are in the pan, heat through, stirring gently, then transfer to a large slow cooker pot. Cover and cook on High for 2–3 hours, stirring once halfway through cooking and again just before serving.

# SAVOURY BAKES

When I was growing up, slow-baked dishes were very popular in Italy; they were often cooked in the wood-fired oven as it cooled down after the bread had been baked. Dishes such as *gattó di patate* and *timballo di riso* could be left in the low oven to cook for a long time, sometimes all day, ready for the evening meal.

People who didn't have an oven at home would bring their savoury dishes to the local bakery to put in the hot ovens once the day's bread was all made; the dishes would be left for most of the day and collected later, nicely cooked and warm –
and all for free!

This method of cooking was traditionally used on the eve of the feast of All Saints – these days known as Hallowe'en. Food was cooked during the day and night, but tradition dictated that it was forbidden to cook on 1 November; that day was dedicated to visiting the cemetery to honour deceased relatives and families needed a warm cooked meal ready upon their return from the cemetery.

Most of the bakes in this chapter can be made in advance and reheated when required; some can also be enjoyed cold. Many are meals in themselves and are ideal to serve at parties.

# Patate alla birra

## Potato bake with beer

A light, simple potato dish, ideal to accompany roast meats – or it can be eaten as a meal by itself. The subtle taste of malt in the beer marries really well with the potatoes, onions and smoked bacon. This can be made a day in advance and reheated.

Serves 4–6

1kg/2lb 4oz potatoes, peeled and
   thinly sliced
200ml/7fl oz/scant 1 cup lager beer
2 tbsp extra virgin olive oil
salt and freshly ground black pepper
2 large onions, thinly sliced
200g/7oz smoked bacon cubes
85g/3oz pecorino (romano)
   cheese, grated

Preheat the oven to 200°C/400°F/gas mark 6.

Put the potatoes in a large bowl and toss together with the beer, olive oil, salt and pepper.

Lift the potatoes out of the beer mixture and line the bottom of an ovenproof dish with a layer of potatoes, followed by a layer of sliced onions; sprinkle over a few cubes of bacon and some of the grated pecorino. Continue layering in the same way until all the ingredients are used, finishing with grated pecorino. Pour over the beer mixture, cover with foil and bake in the oven for 1 hour. Remove the foil and bake for another 30 minutes.

Remove from the oven and leave to rest for a couple of minutes before serving.

# Cipolle ripiene
## Baked filled onions

Onions are perfect for slow cooking – their flavour becomes delicate and subtle. They can be filled with all sorts of different ingredients; I love this combination of mortadella, walnuts and thyme, which I sometimes use as a stuffing for chicken. This dish can be eaten by itself, served with a green salad, or as an accompaniment to roast meat. It can be made in advance and reheated when needed.

Serves 2–4

Preheat the oven to 180°C/350°F/gas mark 4.

4 large onions
115g/4oz mortadella, finely chopped
85g/3oz/¾ cup walnuts, finely chopped
85g/3oz Parmesan, grated
1 tsp finely chopped thyme leaves
salt and freshly ground black pepper
2 eggs, beaten
extra virgin olive oil, to drizzle
2 tbsp dried breadcrumbs
100ml/3½fl oz/scant ½ cup
    vegetable stock (see page 36)
    – or use a stock cube

Peel the onions and slice off the tops at about a third of the way down, then scoop out the cavities. Finely chop the scooped-out onion and combine with the mortadella, walnuts, Parmesan, thyme, some salt and pepper and the eggs; set aside.

Put the onions in an ovenproof dish and sprinkle a little salt and pepper inside them. Fill each onion with the mortadella mixture, drizzle with a little olive oil and sprinkle with the breadcrumbs. Pour the stock into the bottom of the dish, cover with foil and bake in the oven for 1 hour. Remove the foil and bake for another 15 minutes.

Remove from the oven and leave to rest for 5 minutes before serving.

# Gattó di patate con porcini e speck

## Mashed potato cake with porcini and speck

The *gattó di patate* is a typically Neapolitan dish whose name derives from the French *gâteau*, meaning 'cake'. Apparently it was first made in Naples in 1768 for the wedding of Marie Caroline (sister of Marie Antoinette) to Ferdinand, King of Naples; French cuisine was highly influential in Europe at that time. In southern Italy, *gattó* is traditionally made with mozzarella and pieces of leftover salami and prosciutto. This is a south-meets-north version, a southern speciality using northern ingredients – dried porcini mushrooms, speck (smoked cured ham) and Taleggio cheese. Of course, if you prefer, you can use mozzarella and a mix of prosciutto and salami. Once baked, it is left to rest in the warm oven for at least 30 minutes – this way all the flavours come together for maximum taste – and enjoyed at room temperature. It tastes even better the next day, eaten cold. This is a meal in itself, served with a mixed side salad.

Serves 4–6

1kg/2lb 4oz floury (starchy) potatoes, such as red Desirée, scrubbed
100g/3½oz/7 tbsp butter, plus extra to grease
150g/5½oz piece of speck or Parma ham, cubed
100g/3½oz Parmesan, grated
2 eggs
2 egg yolks
salt and freshly ground black pepper
3 tbsp dried breadcrumbs, plus extra to dust
3 tbsp extra virgin olive oil
2 garlic cloves, crushed
40g/1½oz dried porcini mushrooms, soaked in warm water for 20 minutes
85g/3oz button mushrooms, halved
1 tbsp chopped fresh parsley
200g/7oz Taleggio cheese, roughly chopped

Boil the potatoes in their skins until cooked through, drain, leave until cool enough to handle, then peel off the skins. Mash the potatoes together with 75g/2¾oz/5 tbsp of the butter. Add the speck, Parmesan, eggs and yolks and combine well. Season with salt and pepper to taste. Set aside.

Preheat the oven to 180°C/350°F/gas mark 4. Grease an ovenproof dish with butter and dust with breadcrumbs.

Heat the olive oil in a frying pan, add the garlic and cook on a medium heat for a couple of minutes, then discard the garlic. Drain the porcini, add to the pan and stir-fry for 4 minutes. Add the button mushrooms, parsley, salt and pepper to taste and cook for a further 2 minutes. Remove from the heat and set aside.

Put half of the mashed potato mixture in the prepared dish, cover with the mushroom mixture and the Taleggio cheese, and then the remaining potato mixture. Dot with the remaining butter and sprinkle with breadcrumbs. Bake in the oven for 1 hour, until the top is golden brown.

Switch the oven off and leave to rest for at least 30 minutes before serving.

# Tiella Pugliese con cozze

## Baked rice with mussels

This typical peasant dish from Puglia, the heel of Italy, is said to have Spanish influences. It was often made with 'poor', but nourishing, local ingredients, to easily and cheaply feed a large family at the end of a long working day in the fields. It is unclear whether the word *tiella* derives from the dish it was cooked in or the cooking method. No matter; it has over time become the name of this dish, of which there are many variations, made with vegetables, meat or fish, depending on availability. However, the two main ingredients, rice and potatoes, are always present. This version using mussels comes from Bari, the capital city of the Puglia region. The uncooked rice is scattered over the layers of ingredients and the end result is an interesting type of baked risotto with a lovely subtle seafood flavour.

Serves 4

250g/9oz fresh mussels, scrubbed, any open or broken shells discarded
2 handfuls of parsley, finely chopped, plus extra to serve
1 garlic clove, finely chopped
1 onion, finely sliced
salt and freshly ground black pepper
100ml/3½fl oz/scant ½ cup extra virgin olive oil
250g/9oz potatoes, peeled and thinly sliced
250g/9oz cherry tomatoes, halved
10g/¼oz pecorino (romano) cheese, grated
150g/5½oz/¾ cup arborio rice

Preheat the oven to 170°C/325°F/gas mark 3.

Put the mussels in a pan, cover with a lid and cook on a high heat for a couple of minutes until the shells open. Remove from the heat and leave to cool slightly, discarding any mussels whose shells remain closed. Combine the parsley and garlic and set aside.

Line an ovenproof dish with the sliced onion, followed by half of the parsley mixture, sprinkle with salt and pepper and drizzle with 2 tablespoons olive oil. Cover with half of the potatoes, the mussels, tomatoes, 2 tablespoons olive oil and the remaining parsley mixture. Sprinkle with the pecorino, then scatter in the raw rice, the remaining potatoes and the remaining olive oil. Pour in 400ml/14fl oz/1⅔ cups water, ensuring you cover all the ingredients – you may need less or more water.

Cover with foil and bake for 1¼ hours, until the potatoes are very tender when pierced with a skewer. Serve hot, sprinkled with parsley.

# Calamari ripieni
## Filled baked squid

I love squid and whenever I'm on the coast in Italy, whether at a restaurant or at my sister's house, I make sure to have them – in a salad, stewed with tomatoes, in pasta, or filled and slow-baked like this. Made this way, they are ideal as a light lunch served with a side salad.

Serves 4

4 large squid (calamari),
    including tentacles
3 tbsp extra virgin olive oil, plus
    extra to drizzle
2 garlic cloves, finely chopped
4 anchovy fillets
1 tbsp capers
200ml/7fl oz/scant 1 cup white wine
salt and freshly ground black pepper
100g/3½oz bread, finely chopped
40g/1½oz/5 tbsp pine nuts
grated zest of ½ lemon
1 tbsp chopped fresh parsley

Thoroughly clean the calamari – you can ask your fishmonger to do this – ending up with four perfect sack-like calamari ready to fill. Roughly chop about half of the tentacles and set aside.

Preheat the oven to 180°C/350°F/gas mark 4. Lightly oil a baking dish.

Heat the olive oil in a saucepan, add the garlic, anchovies and capers and sweat for a few minutes, stirring with a wooden spoon until the anchovies have dissolved. Add the chopped tentacles and stir-fry for about 5 minutes, then add the wine and allow to evaporate; season with salt and pepper to taste. Remove from the heat and leave to cool.

Stir in the bread, pine nuts, lemon zest and parsley. Fill each squid with this mixture and tuck the reserved tentacles into the ends, place in the baking dish, drizzle with extra virgin olive oil, cover with foil and bake in the oven for 45 minutes. Remove the foil and bake for another 15 minutes, until lightly golden. Serve hot.

# Peperoni al forno ripieni al risotto
## Baked peppers filled with risotto

I love roasted peppers, and this nutritious filling makes them a healthy complete meal. Filling peppers with rice is quite common in Mediterranean countries, but I find they can be a little bland; I have made a quick risotto with some summer vegetables to use as the stuffing and the addition of mint gives a pleasant refreshing flavour. You can make this dish very colourful by using red, yellow, green and orange peppers. I have suggested one pepper per person, but if, like me, you are greedy, double the quantities – you can always enjoy them cold or heated up the next day.

Serves 4

2 tbsp extra virgin olive oil, plus
   extra to drizzle
½ onion, finely chopped
150g/5½oz/¾ cup arborio rice
½ courgette (zucchini), cubed
½ aubergine (eggplant), cubed
2 tsp tomato purée (paste)
700ml/1¼ pints/3 cups hot vegetable
   stock (see page 36) – or use a
   stock cube
30g/1oz Parmesan, grated
salt and freshly ground black pepper
4 large (bell) peppers
1 ball of mozzarella
   (about 125g/4½oz),cubed
a handful of fresh mint leaves, torn

Preheat the oven to 180°C/350°F/gas mark 4. Heat the olive oil in a saucepan, add the onion and sweat on a medium heat until softened. Stir in the rice until each grain is coated with oil. Stir in the courgette, aubergine and tomato purée, then add a little stock and cook until absorbed.

Gradually add the remaining stock, stirring all the time, for 12–15 minutes. The rice should still be quite firm. Remove from the heat, stir in the Parmesan, taste for seasoning and leave to cool slightly.

Slice the tops off the peppers, keeping the stems so they look like little hats, and set aside. Put the peppers in a lightly oiled baking dish. Half-fill them with the risotto, add a few cubes of mozzarella, gently pressing it into the filling, and some mint. Add the remaining risotto and more mozzarella, pressing it in. Put the 'hats' on the filled peppers, drizzle with a little olive oil, cover with foil and bake for 45 minutes. Remove the foil and bake for another 15 minutes.

Remove from the oven and leave to rest for 5 minutes before serving. Can also be enjoyed cold.

# V

# Timballo di riso estivo
## Baked rice with peppers, aubergines and tomato

A light rice dish slowly baked in the oven together with summer vegetables. You can roast the peppers in advance: place in a hot oven until the skins blacken, remove from the oven and leave until cool; the skins will easily come off. You can also grill the aubergines in advance, either under a hot grill (broiler) or on a hot griddle pan. Once the vegetables are cool, put them in the fridge until required. The *timballo* can be eaten warm or enjoyed cold the next day.

Serves 4

250g/9oz/1¼ cups arborio rice
salt and freshly ground black pepper
400g/14oz aubergine (eggplant),
   thinly sliced, grilled (see above)
4 tbsp extra virgin olive oil
1 small yellow (bell) pepper, roasted
   and peeled (see above)
1 small red (bell) pepper, roasted and
   peeled (see above)
400g/14oz tomatoes: half roughly
   chopped, half thinly sliced
1 garlic clove, finely chopped
small handful of parsley, roughly
   chopped
8 basil leaves, roughly torn
150g/5½oz mozzarella, roughly sliced

Preheat the oven to 170°C/325°F/gas mark 3. Bring a saucepan of lightly salted water to the boil and cook the rice for 8 minutes. Drain and leave to cool.

Lightly brush the grilled aubergine slices with olive oil and set aside.

Roughly chop the roasted peppers, place on a plate, sprinkle with salt and drizzle with olive oil.

Place the chopped tomatoes in a bowl and combine with the garlic, parsley, basil, a generous tablespoon of olive oil, some salt and pepper and leave to marinate for 10 minutes. Stir in the cold cooked rice.

Lightly grease an ovenproof dish with olive oil and line with the aubergines. Add half of the rice mixture, followed by the peppers, mozzarella and a few tomato slices, then the remaining rice mixture. Put the remaining tomato slices on top, drizzle with olive oil, cover with foil and bake for 50 minutes. Remove the foil and bake for another 5 minutes.

Remove from the oven and leave to rest for 5 minutes before serving. Can also be enjoyed cold.

# Patate al forno tartufate
## 'Posh' baked potatoes

When I was a child, I remember that once all the baking was done in the wood-fired oven, my grandfather would often throw in a few potatoes – so as not to 'waste' the heat and ash. The result was a delicious hot potato, which we would eat as a treat with just a little salt. It was not until I arrived in England that I realized baked potatoes were very popular with all sorts of fillings. Potatoes and truffle marry really well together, so why not combine the humble spud with decadent truffle for a real treat?

Serves 4

4 baking potatoes
salt and freshly ground black pepper
5 tsp truffle oil
40g/1½oz Parmesan, grated
100g/3½oz fontina cheese, grated
1 tsp thyme, very finely chopped

Preheat the oven to 200°C/400°F/gas mark 6.

Wash and dry the potatoes, prick them all over with a fork or skewer, then rub all over with salt and a little of the truffle oil – about 1 teaspoon should be enough for all the potatoes. Wrap each potato in foil and bake in the oven for about 1¼ hours, until cooked through.

Remove from the oven, slice or cut the tops off the potatoes and carefully spoon out most of the soft potato into a bowl. Mix the spooned-out potato with truffle oil, Parmesan, fontina, thyme and some salt and pepper. Put the filling back in the skins and return to the oven for a few minutes to allow the cheese to melt. Serve hot.

Vg

# Carote al forno con erbe
## Baked herby carrots

Simple to prepare, baked carrots infused with herbs are a wonderful way to serve this popular root vegetable. This is an ideal accompaniment to main courses, especially roast meats. If you prefer to keep the carrots whole you will need to increase the cooking time.

Serves 4

2 shallots, finely sliced
1 celery stalk, roughly chopped
500g/1lb 2oz carrots, cut into
  large chunks
2 tbsp extra virgin olive oil, plus
  extra to drizzle
salt and freshly ground black pepper
2 bay leaves
3 sprigs of thyme
8 sage leaves
2 tbsp finely chopped fresh parsley
150ml/5fl oz/⅔ cup vegetable stock
  (see page 36) – or use a stock cube

Preheat the oven to 180°C/350°F/gas mark 4. Put the shallots and celery in an ovenproof dish and put the carrots on top.

In a bowl, combine the olive oil, salt and pepper and pour over the carrots. Scatter with the herbs and pour over the stock. Leave to infuse for about 15 minutes.

Cover with foil and bake in the oven for 1 hour. Remove the foil, drizzle with extra virgin olive oil and bake for another 15 minutes. Remove from the oven and leave to rest for 5 minutes before serving.

# ROASTS &
# POT
# ROASTS

I love the smell of roasted meat slowly cooking in the oven – just by the smell I know it's a Sunday morning. Since living in England, I have become accustomed to enjoying a 'roast dinner' and look forward to the weekly ritual, whether it's traditional roast beef and Yorkshire pudding, pork with apple sauce or a stuffed roast chicken, all served with lovely roast potatoes and vegetables.

Italians enjoy roasts too, but as they tend to be served after a *primo* (first course) of perhaps pasta or risotto, there is less need for so many accompaniments and the meat is often simply served with a salad. Classic Italian roasts of beef, veal, pork and lamb tend to be laden with herbs, which really enhance the flavour of the meat; my *Arrosto di manzo alle erbe* (see page 128) is a good example.

Oven roasting is a very similar process to spit roasting – cooking meat over an open fire – which has been done since ancient times. Spit roasting ensured that no part of the meat dried out as it turned on the spit and fat and juices ran over the surface of the meat. Spit roasting whole lambs, goats and pigs remains popular in Sardinia. *Porceddu* (suckling pig) infused with local myrtle leaves is cooked in this way in rural areas of the island and for celebrations like weddings. Another ancient method still used in inland parts of Sardinia is *incarralzadu*, in which the animal is cooked underground in a large hole and a fire made above. Sardinians have always been very traditional in their ways, probably because of their island location, and this way of cooking is still very much alive and celebrated today.

Oven roasting, where the heat takes a long time to reach the centre of the food, is mostly used to cook tender joints of meat. Pot-roasting allows you to

use tougher, more economical, cuts of meat and is very popular in Italy; in this method, a large piece of meat is first browned, then cooked slowly with liquid. Both methods are very simple: once in the pot or roasting tin, you can more or less leave the meat to its own devices – just remember to baste the oven joint and ensure there is enough liquid for the pot roast.

# Arrosto di manzo alle erbe

## Roast beef with herbs

Delicious, easy to prepare, full of the fresh flavour of herbs, roast beef Italian-style is the perfect Sunday lunch. Italians usually enjoy a first course of pasta or risotto followed by the roast beef served with a simple salad.

Serves 4–6

2 carrots, sliced lengthways
1.4kg/3lb 2oz topside of beef
100ml/3½fl oz/scant ½ cup extra
    virgin olive oil
3 garlic cloves, finely chopped
needles from 3 sprigs of rosemary,
    finely chopped
small bunch of thyme, finely chopped
2 tbsp finely chopped marjoram
a handful of parsley, finely chopped
salt and freshly ground black pepper

Preheat the oven to 200°C/400°F/gas mark 6.

Put the carrots in a roasting tin and place the beef on top (this prevents the meat from sticking to the tin). Combine the olive oil, garlic, herbs, salt and pepper and pour over the meat, rubbing well. Roast in the oven for 20 minutes, then cover with foil and continue to roast for 1¼ hours, turning the meat over after 30 minutes.

Remove from the oven and leave to rest for 10 minutes. Slice and serve.

**Vg**

# Zucca ripiena arrostita
## Whole roasted and filled pumpkin

This is a wonderful way of cooking a pumpkin or squash whole. Packed with nutritious vegetables and spelt, it makes a delicious main course dish. The way the spelt is cooked with the vegetables is the same method you'd use when making risotto: as the spelt absorbs the stock, you keep adding more stock until the spelt is cooked through. I love Delica pumpkins, but you could use other types of squash to make this dish, too.

Serves 4

1 Delica pumpkin
    (approx. 1.5kg /3lb 5oz)
4 tbsp extra virgin olive oil, plus
    extra for drizzling
needles from 2 small sprigs of
    rosemary, finely chopped
leaves from 4 sprigs of thyme,
    finely chopped
1 garlic clove, diced
½ red chilli, finely chopped
1 small red onion, finely chopped
2 carrots – 1 finely chopped and the
    other sliced in half lengthways
1 small parsnip, finely chopped
1 celery stalk, finely chopped
½ leek, finely chopped
200g/7oz/scant ½ cup chestnut
    mushrooms, roughly chopped
150g/5½oz/scant ¾ cup spelt
25g/1oz/scant ¼ cup walnuts,
    roughly chopped
75ml/2½fl oz/scant ⅓ cup white wine
½ tbsp tomato purée (paste)
750ml/1¼ pints/3 cups hot vegetable
    stock (see page 36) – or use a
    stock cube

Preheat the oven to 200°C/400°F/gas mark 6.

Take the Delica pumpkin and, using a sharp knife, carefully remove the top so you are left with a 'lid'. Scoop out the seeds inside and discard. If any of the flesh comes away, roughly chop it and set aside.

Heat the olive oil in a large, deep frying pan and sweat the herbs, garlic, chilli, onion, chopped carrot, parsnip, celery, leek, mushrooms and any pumpkin flesh on a medium heat for 10 minutes, until softened.

Stir in the spelt and walnuts, then increase the heat, add the white wine and cook until absorbed. Stir in the tomato purée and a ladleful of hot stock, stirring well until the liquid is absorbed again. Add more hot stock and continue cooking in this way, like you would when making risotto, for about 15 minutes until the spelt is cooked.

Drizzle a little olive oil into a roasting tin, then place the carrot halves inside and the Delica pumpkin on top – this creates a sort of base preventing the pumpkin from sticking to the tin. Drizzle the inside of the pumpkin with a little oil and sprinkling of salt, then fill with the spelt mixture. Cover with the pumpkin 'lid' and roast in the oven for 1 hour.

After 30 minutes, reduce the temperature to 180°C/350°F/gas mark 4. 10 minutes before the end of the cooking time, remove the lid and let it cook in the roasting tin, flesh-side up.

Remove the pumpkin from the oven and leave it to rest for a couple of minutes, then slice and serve.

# Brasato al Barolo

## Braised beef in Barolo wine

This classic Piemontese dish, made with the region's famous Barolo wine, is fit for a king. It can, of course, be made with other, less expensive, full-bodied red wines, but for a special occasion I like to use Barolo. The meat is first marinated overnight with vegetables, herbs and wine before being slow-cooked with the same ingredients, giving the meat its richness. Delicious served with polenta (cornmeal), as is traditional in Piedmont, and also good with mashed potatoes.

Serves 4

1kg/2lb 4oz shoulder/blade or
   topside of beef
4 tbsp extra virgin olive oil
30g/1oz/2 tbsp butter
salt and freshly ground black pepper

**for the marinade**
1 garlic clove, left whole
2 bay leaves
2 sprigs of rosemary
8 black peppercorns
1 large onion, finely sliced
2 celery stalks, finely chopped
1 bottle of Barolo wine

Gently dry the beef with kitchen paper, then put it in a bowl together with all the marinade ingredients. Cover with clingfilm (plastic wrap) and leave in the fridge for 12 hours or overnight.

Remove the meat from the marinade and pat dry with kitchen paper. Strain the marinade, reserving the liquid, vegetables and herbs.

Heat the oil and butter in a large flameproof pot, add the beef and brown well all over. Remove and set aside. In the same pot, add the vegetables and herbs from the marinade and sweat on a medium heat for about 3 minutes. Return the meat to the pan, add some salt and pepper and cook on a medium heat for 5 minutes. Increase the heat, add the wine from the marinade and bring to the boil, then reduce the heat to low, partially cover with a lid and cook gently for 2½ hours, until the meat is tender, turning the meat over from time to time.

Remove the meat and set aside. Increase the heat and cook the sauce for about 5 minutes, until it has reduced slightly. Slice the meat and serve with the vegetables and sauce, with polenta or mashed potatoes.

---

**For a slow cooker**

Marinate the beef. Drain and brown as above. Lift the beef out of the pan and put into a medium slow cooker pot. Sweat the vegetables and herbs from the marinade, then add the marinade, salt and pepper, bring to the boil then pour over the beef.

Cover with a lid and cook on High for 4 hours, turning the beef once, then reduce the heat to Low and cook for 1 hour. Pour the sauce into a saucepan and boil for 15–20 minutes to reduce and thicken. Serve as above.

# Manzo di Rovato all'olio

## Pot-roasted beef with extra virgin olive oil

This ancient dish, originating from the town of Rovato in Lombardy, northern Italy, is about 500 years old. At the time it was a dish cooked for the wealthy: they could afford not only meat but also 'exotic' ingredients such as anchovies and capers brought to Rovato by merchants travelling from Venice to Milan. The meat used for this dish is known in Italy as *cappello del prete* (priest's hat), which is a triangular cut of beef from the outer part of the shoulder, ideally suited to slow cooking; chuck eye is the nearest equivalent and a good butcher should be able to provide it. The olive oil is an important part of the dish, so please do use good-quality extra virgin. The extra sauce can be served the next day with some runny polenta.

Serves 4

200ml/7fl oz/scant 1 cup extra
   virgin olive oil
1.2kg/2lb 10oz chuck eye or chuck
   beef joint or feather steak
2 tbsp capers, rinsed
4 anchovy fillets
2 onions, finely chopped
1 celery stalk, finely chopped
3 carrots, finely chopped
500ml/18fl oz/2 cups dry white wine
3 courgettes (zucchini), sliced
30g/1oz Parmesan, grated
20g/¾oz/scant ¼ cup dried breadcrumbs
salt and freshly ground black pepper

Heat the olive oil in a large flameproof pot, add the beef and brown well on all sides on a high heat. Add the capers and anchovies and cook on a medium heat, stirring with a wooden spoon until the anchovies have dissolved. Stir in the onions, celery and carrots, pour in the wine, cover with a lid and cook on a low heat for 1 hour.

Add the courgettes and continue to cook for a further 1 hour.

Remove the meat from the pot and set aside. Using a food processor or blender, blend the vegetables and liquid until smooth. Stir in the Parmesan and breadcrumbs and season with salt and pepper to taste. Slice the meat and serve with the sauce.

---

**For a slow cooker**

Brown the meat, add the capers, anchovies and vegetables as above, then add 400ml/14fl oz/1⅔ cups of wine. Bring to the boil, then transfer everything to a large slow cooker pot. Cover and cook on High for 4 hours. Turn the beef over, then add the sliced courgettes and cook on Low for 1–1½ hours. Blend the sauce and serve as above.

# Braciolone Palermitano

## Filled rolled beef cooked in tomato sauce

This traditional southern Italian Sunday lunch dish is one of my favourites and very reminiscent of my childhood. Each region makes its own version and my family would make it with local cheese and salami. This is a Sicilian version, hence the Italian title, using caciocavallo cheese; if you can't find it in your Italian deli, you can substitute provolone, pecorino (romano) or Parmesan. Beef brisket is ideal for slow cooking and the tasty filling turns this economical cut of meat into a meal fit for a king. Italians usually serve the tomato sauce with pasta for a starter and the meat as a main course with a green salad. If you have leftover tomato sauce, you can freeze it for another time.

Serves 4–6

700g/1lb 9oz beef brisket
2 slices of mortadella
3 tbsp extra virgin olive oil
1 small onion, finely chopped
100g/3½oz fresh breadcrumbs
50g/1¾oz caciocavallo cheese, grated
70g/2½oz salami, finely chopped
20g/¾oz sultanas (golden raisins),
    soaked in lukewarm water to
    soften, drained
20g/¾oz/generous 2 tbsp pine nuts
a handful of parsley, roughly chopped
salt and freshly ground black pepper

**for the sauce**
3 tbsp extra virgin olive oil
1 small onion
a handful of basil leaves
175ml/6fl oz/¾ cup red wine
1 tbsp tomato purée (paste), diluted
    with a little lukewarm water
1kg/2lb 4oz tomato passata
    (strained tomatoes)

Put the beef flat on a board. Make a cut halfway through the centre of the meat, then carefully slice horizontally through both sides of the meat so that it opens out like a book. Flatten slightly with a meat tenderizer, line with the mortadella slices and set aside.

Heat the olive oil in a saucepan, add the onion and sweat until softened. Stir in the breadcrumbs until all the oil has been absorbed, remove from the heat and leave to cool. Add the cheese, salami, sultanas, pine nuts and parsley and combine well together. Season with salt and pepper to taste. Spread the mixture over the mortadella. Carefully roll the meat and tie securely with kitchen string to ensure the filling does not escape. Set aside.

To make the sauce, heat the olive oil in a large flameproof pot, add the meat and brown well on all sides. Add the onion and sweat until softened. Stir in the basil leaves, add the wine and allow to evaporate, then add the diluted tomato purée, passata, and salt and pepper to taste. Bring to the boil, reduce the heat, cover with a lid and cook on a low heat for 3 hours. Halfway through cooking, very carefully turn the meat over, and from time to time baste the meat with the tomato sauce.

Carefully remove the meat from the sauce, place on a serving dish, discard the string and carve into slices, serving with a little of the sauce. Use the remaining sauce to dress freshly cooked pasta.

# Pastizada alla Veneta
## Venetian pot roast

This classic Venetian pot-roast, traditionally made with horsemeat, is slow-cooking at its best; the meat is left to marinate overnight in vinegar and spices before being slow-cooked with a little white wine, Marsala and the spices from the marinade. The end result is very tender beef with the aromatic flavour of the spices. Carve fairly thick slices, otherwise the beef will fall apart. Serve with runny polenta (cornmeal) for a hearty Venetian meal.

Serves 4

1.5kg/3lb 5oz topside of beef
100ml/3½fl oz/scant ½ cup extra
    virgin olive oil
1 onion, finely chopped
salt and freshly ground black pepper
4 tbsp dry white wine
4 tbsp Marsala wine
200ml/7fl oz/scant 1 cup beef stock
    (see page 25) or vegetable stock
    (see page 36)

**for the marinade**
500ml/18fl oz/2 cups red wine vinegar
2 garlic cloves, left whole
2 celery stalks, sliced
2 sprigs of rosemary
2 cloves
a pinch of ground cinnamon
a pinch of salt
6 black peppercorns

Combine the marinade ingredients, pour over the beef, cover with clingfilm (plastic wrap) and leave in the fridge to marinate overnight.

Remove the meat from the marinade, pat dry with kitchen paper and set aside. Strain the marinade, reserving the vegetables and herbs. Cut a piece of greaseproof (waxed) paper slightly larger than the diameter of your cooking pot and lightly grease.

Heat the olive oil in a flameproof pot, add the onion and the vegetables from the marinade and sweat on a medium heat for 5 minutes. Remove the vegetables and set aside. Add the beef and brown well all over; season with salt and pepper. Add the wine, Marsala and stock, reduce the heat, then cover with the greaseproof paper and the lid and cook on a gentle heat for 2½ hours.

Remove the meat and set aside on a board. Pass the sauce through a fine sieve into a small pan and, using a small whisk, beat the sauce so it is well amalgamated. Carve the meat into thick slices, pour over the sauce and serve with runny polenta.

# Stufato di manzo alla Siciliana

## Sicilian pot roast

This recipe evolved from memories of a pasta dish I once enjoyed in Sicily. To the pesto of almonds and olives, I added a hint of cinnamon, giving it that subtle North African flavour which is so often present in Sicilian dishes. Once the pesto is inserted into the beef, the meat is left to slow cook in stock. Delicious served with couscous or steamed rice.

Serves 4

70g/2½oz green olives, finely chopped
70g/2½oz flaked almonds,
   finely chopped
½ tsp ground cinnamon
salt and freshly ground black pepper
800g/1lb 12oz beef brisket
3 tbsp extra virgin olive oil
1 onion, finely chopped
1 garlic clove, finely chopped
a handful of parsley, finely chopped
2 tbsp tomato purée (paste)
100ml/3½fl oz/scant ½ cup red wine
700ml/1¼ pints/3 cups hot beef stock
   (see page 25) – or use a stock cube

Combine the olives, almonds, cinnamon, salt and pepper. Make incisions all over the beef with a skewer or sharp knife and insert the mixture well inside, also placing some between the meat and the outer fat; if the filling looks as though it might fall out, tie the meat securely with kitchen string.

Heat the olive oil in a flameproof pot and brown the beef on all sides. Add the onion, garlic and parsley and sweat for a couple of minutes. Mix the tomato purée with the wine and add to the meat, together with the stock. Bring to the boil, reduce the heat, cover with a lid and cook gently for 3 hours, until the meat is tender and cooked through.

Remove the meat and set aside. Increase the heat and cook the sauce for a few minutes, without a lid, until it has reduced and thickened slightly. Slice the meat and serve with the sauce, and a dish of couscous or rice.

---

**For a slow cooker**

Make up the recipe as above and bring to the boil, then transfer everything to a medium slow cooker pot. Cover and cook on High for 5 hours, turning the meat over once during cooking. If you are not ready to serve the beef, then reduce the heat to Low and cook for up to 1 hour. Serve as above.

# Porchetta natalizia

## Festive stuffed pork belly

I love making porchetta and often make a large one for special occasions or when I have lots of guests. It can be made in advance and sliced when required, and is delicious eaten cold. The traditional porchetta, popular street food in the region of Rome, is a whole piglet, cooked on a spit, sliced thickly and served as a substantial sandwich. To enrich the porchetta further, I have added a filling of minced pork and chicken livers. It's an unusual cut of pork and you will need to order the meat from your butcher in advance, but it is surprisingly simple to prepare.

Serves 4-6

3kg/6lb 8oz jacket of pork
  (loin and belly, boned)
salt and freshly ground black pepper
5 tbsp vin santo
grated zest of 2 lemons
2 tbsp extra virgin olive oil, plus
  extra to rub
1 onion, finely chopped
175g/6oz minced (ground) pork
175g/6oz chicken livers, finely chopped
350g/12oz bread, soaked in
  lukewarm water
10 sage leaves, roughly chopped
needles from 2 sprigs of rosemary,
  roughly chopped
leaves from 2 sprigs of thyme
15g/½oz/2 tbsp pine nuts
30g/1oz/3 tbsp sultanas
6 slices of mortadella

Unroll the jacket of pork and lay it on a board, skin side down. Season and rub well into the meat. Drizzle the vin santo and sprinkle the lemon zest over and massage in well. Roll, wrap in clingfilm (plastic wrap) and rest in the fridge for 30 minutes.

Meanwhile, heat the olive oil in a pan and sweat the onion for a couple of minutes. Add the minced pork and brown, stirring well, then add the chicken livers and brown all over. Remove from the heat and leave to cool.

Preheat the oven to 220°C/425°F/gas mark 7. Lightly grease a roasting dish with olive oil.

Squeeze the excess water from the bread and chop finely. Add the bread to the cooled meat, together with the herbs, pine nuts and sultanas and mix well.

Discarding the clingfilm, open out the pork on a board. Line with 3 slices of mortadella, add the stuffing and top with the remaining mortadella. Carefully roll up the meat and tie securely with string. Massage all over with olive oil, salt and pepper and place in the roasting dish. Roast in the oven for 30 minutes.

Cover the meat with foil, turn the oven down to 150°C/300°F/gas mark 2 and continue to roast for 3 hours. Remove the foil, turn off the oven and leave to rest in the oven until it cools down.

You can serve immediately, carved into slices, or serve cold later. It will keep for up to a week wrapped in foil in the fridge.

# Stinco di maiale all'arancia

## Roasted pork shins with oranges

*Stinco* (shin or shank) is popular throughout Italy, both for slow roasting and, in the case of pork shins, also for curing into salami and sausages. When buying pork shanks, bear in mind that although they look quite large, the majority of the weight consists of bone, so one shank has only enough meat for two people. The meat is well suited to long, slow cooking and the fact that it is on the bone makes this pork cut extremely tasty. The addition of oranges really brings out the flavour of the meat in this simple-to-prepare and unusual Sunday roast.

Serves 4

2 pork shins, about 1.5kg/3lb 5oz each
salt and freshly ground black pepper
4 tbsp extra virgin olive oil
2 red onions, finely sliced
2 carrots, sliced lengthways
2 sprigs of rosemary
400ml/14fl oz/1⅔ cups dry white wine
300ml/10fl oz/1¼ cups vegetable stock
 (see page 36) – or use a stock cube
4 oranges, plus grated zest and juice
 of 2 oranges
125g/4½oz/generous ½ cup
 granulated sugar

Preheat the oven to 200°C/400°F/gas mark 6. Put the shins in a roasting tin, rub all over with salt and pepper and drizzle with the olive oil. Roast in the oven for 1 hour.

Add the vegetables, rosemary, wine and stock to the roasting tin and continue to cook for another 1½ hours.

Meanwhile, prepare the oranges and sauce. Peel 4 oranges and cut into 1cm/½-inch slices. Bring some water to the boil in a small pan, add the orange slices, boil for 1 minute, then remove, drain and set aside. Put the juice of 2 oranges in a small pan with the sugar and 125ml/4fl oz/½ cup water and cook on a medium heat, stirring all the time, until the sugar has dissolved. Remove from the heat and set aside.

About 15 minutes before the end of the pork's cooking time, add the orange slices to the roasting tin and pour over the orange sauce.

When the pork shins are cooked, put them on a large serving dish together with the vegetables, orange slices and juices. Sprinkle all over with orange zest and leave to rest for 5 minutes. Carve and serve.

# Lonza di maiale con miele e noci

## Roast pork loin with honey and walnuts

Pork loin is a popular cut for roasting. You can buy it on the bone, with the loin ribs attached, or boneless and tied with string to keep it together. In this recipe I have wrapped pancetta over a boneless joint to keep the pork moist during cooking; the addition of onion, walnuts and honey gives this dish its delicious flavour.

Serves 4

850g/1lb 14oz boneless pork loin joint
extra virgin olive oil, to grease
salt and freshly ground black pepper
6 slices of pancetta or streaky bacon
1 onion, finely sliced
50g/1¾oz walnuts
3 tbsp runny honey
100ml/3½fl oz/scant ½ cup dry
   white wine
100ml/3½fl oz/scant ½ cup hot
   vegetable stock (see page 36)
   – or use a stock cube

Preheat the oven to 150°C/300°F/gas mark 2.

Grease a roasting tin with a little olive oil and add the pork. Rub the pork all over with salt and pepper and arrange slices of pancetta over the meat side of the joint. Roast in the oven for 30 minutes.

Add the onion and walnuts to the roasting tin and brush the honey over the meat. Continue to cook for another 1½ hours, basting with the juices from time to time.

Remove from the oven, put the meat on a board and set aside. Put the roasting tin on a medium heat, add the wine and stir with a wooden spoon until the wine has evaporated. Stir in the hot stock and reduce by half, until the sauce has thickened slightly. Slice the meat and arrange on a serving dish, pour over the sauce and serve.

# Cappone natalizio

## Christmas capon

Capons are castrated roosters; larger than chickens but smaller than turkeys, they are eaten for Christmas in northern Italy, where they are bred specially for this time of year. Traditionally castrated on the day of Saint Rocco (16 August), the capons are then fattened up for four months. During this time they loose their rooster-like qualities, become calmer and more manageable, and develop more tender and succulent flesh. I really like capon and usually have one, stuffed with a mixture of seasonal fruits and nuts, for Christmas lunch.

Serves 6

2kg/4lb 8oz capon
salt and freshly ground black pepper
extra virgin olive oil, to drizzle
8 slices of pancetta

**for the stuffing**
140g/5oz dried apricots, finely chopped
140g/5oz prunes, finely chopped
12 walnuts, finely chopped
300g/10½oz chestnuts, cooked and
  finely chopped
250g/9oz salami, finely chopped
a handful of thyme leaves
140g/5oz bread, soaked in a little
  lukewarm water, drained and
  roughly chopped
50g/1¾oz Parmesan, grated
200ml/7fl oz/scant 1 cup Marsala wine

Preheat the oven to 200°C/400°F/gas mark 6.

Rub salt and pepper all over the capon and inside the cavity and set aside.

Combine all the stuffing ingredients, season with salt and pepper to taste and use to fill the cavity of the capon. Drizzle a little olive oil in a roasting tin, add the capon, cover with pancetta slices and drizzle with a little more olive oil. Cover with foil and roast for 1½ hours, basting with the juices from time to time. Remove the foil and pancetta slices and roast for another 30 minutes or until thoroughly cooked. To test whether the capon is cooked, insert a skewer in the thigh – if the juices run clear, it is done.

Remove from the oven and leave to rest for 10 minutes. Carve and serve with the stuffing.

# Cosciotto d'agnello con piselli e cipolline

## Roast leg of lamb with peas and baby onions

For a special occasion or Sunday lunch, this dish is a must. The combination of baby onions, black olives, anchovies, garlic and peas marry well with the succulent lamb. If you can't find Taggiasca olives, substitute Greek Kalamata olives, which give a distinct tangy taste. For 4 people, half a leg of lamb is sufficient.

Serves 4

1.2kg/2lb 10oz half leg of lamb
salt and freshly ground black pepper
a little extra virgin olive oil
150ml/5fl oz/⅔ cup dry white wine
300g/10½oz baby onions or
    shallots, peeled
24 Taggiasca olives, pitted
2 garlic cloves, left whole, crushed
4 anchovy fillets, roughly chopped
150g/5½oz/generous 1 cup frozen peas

Preheat the oven to 200°C/400°F/gas mark 6. Rub the lamb all over with salt, pepper and a little olive oil. Place in a roasting dish and roast for 20 minutes.

Add half the wine and cook for a further 20 minutes. Add the remaining wine, onions, olives, garlic and anchovies, cover with foil and continue roasting for 1 hour 10 minutes.

Stir in the peas and roast for 10 minutes. Remove the foil and roast for a further 10 minutes.

Remove from the oven and leave to rest for 5 minutes. Put the lamb on a board, carve and serve with the vegetables and juices.

# Anatra arrosto con ripieno di mela e salvia

## Roasted duck with apple and sage

Duck and apple is a perfect marriage, and this dish makes a great alternative for Christmas or for a Sunday lunch. For this recipe, I have used the excellent English Gressingham duck. Keep the drained-off fat and use for roast potatoes to accompany the duck.

Serves 4

1 oven-ready duck, weighing
   about 1.8kg/4lb
salt and freshly ground black pepper
30g/1oz/2 tbsp butter
1 onion
8 sage leaves, finely chopped, plus
   a few extra
3 tbsp fresh breadcrumbs
2 egg yolks
2 Granny Smith apples, peeled,
   cored and roughly chopped
100ml/3½fl oz/scant ½ cup dry
   white wine

Preheat the oven to 180°C/350°F/gas mark 4.

Wipe the duck clean inside and out, season the cavity with salt and pepper and set aside.

Melt the butter in a saucepan, add the onion and sweat on a medium heat for 3 minutes. Add 2 tbsp water and continue to cook for 2 minutes until the onion has softened. Remove from the heat, stir in the chopped sage, breadcrumbs, egg yolks, apples, and some salt and pepper and combine well. Fill the cavity of the duck with this stuffing.

Prick the duck skin all over and sprinkle with salt – this will release the fat and make the duck skin nice and crisp. Put the duck on a rack in a roasting tin and roast for 45 minutes.

Pour off the fat and reserve to make roast potatoes. Drizzle the duck with the wine, scatter with a few sage leaves and continue to roast for about 1¼ hours, until the duck is cooked; test by inserting a skewer in the thigh – if the juices run clear, it is done.

Remove from the oven, pour off the fat and leave to rest for 5–10 minutes. Carve and serve with the stuffing.

# Pollo ubriaco con peperoni

## Boozy baked chicken with peppers

This is a really simple dish to prepare: put all your ingredients in a roasting dish and pop in the oven to do the rest. All the flavours infuse together and the alcohol and mustard give the chicken a real kick! Excellent for an easy Sunday lunch or midweek meal served with steamed rice.

Serves 4

150ml/5fl oz/⅔ cup dry white wine
1 tbsp English mustard
850g/1lb 14oz chicken thighs
   and drumsticks
100g/3½oz prosciutto, roughly chopped
10 baby onions or shallots, peeled
225g/8oz baby vine tomatoes, halved
1 yellow (bell) pepper, thinly sliced
1 red (bell) pepper, thinly sliced
2 garlic cloves, left whole
salt and freshly ground black pepper
2 tbsp port
2 tbsp brandy
2 tbsp extra virgin olive oil
1 tbsp chopped fresh parsley

Combine the wine and mustard and set aside.

Put the chicken pieces in an ovenproof dish with the prosciutto, onions, tomatoes, peppers and garlic, sprinkle with salt and pepper and toss together. Pour over the white wine mixture, port, brandy and olive oil and toss again. Cover with foil and set aside for the flavours to infuse for 20 minutes. Preheat the oven to 170°C/325°F/gas mark 3.

Place in the oven and bake for 1 hour, basting from time to time. Remove the foil and continue to cook for another 30 minutes.

Remove from the oven, garnish with parsley and serve.

# Vg

# Verdure miste arrostite
## Mixed roasted root vegetables

When I cook roasted meat or poultry, I like to make a tray of roasted vegetables as an accompaniment. I usually put in whatever vegetables are lying around, toss them with some extra virgin olive oil, seasoning and herbs and slow-roast them in the wood-fired oven. I tend not to peel vegetables like potatoes and carrots because a lot of essential nutrients are in the skin, but I leave it to you. You can use whatever root vegetables you like: if you don't have celeriac, for example, use extra carrots or parsnips. In warmer months, I use vegetables such as peppers, courgettes (zucchini), aubergines (eggplants) and baby new potatoes.

Serves 4

4 large potatoes, scrubbed and cut
　　into quarters
2 large carrots, scrubbed and cut in
　　half lengthways
2 parsnips, peeled and cut in half
　　lengthways
300g/10½oz celeriac (celery root),
　　peeled and cut into large chunks
2 fennel bulbs, halved or quartered
　　depending on size
2 red onions, peeled, halved or
　　quartered depending on size
8 tbsp extra virgin olive oil
salt and freshly ground black pepper
2 sprigs of rosemary
2 sprigs of thyme
2 bay leaves

Preheat the oven to 200°C/400°F/gas mark 6.

Put all the vegetables in a large roasting tin, toss with extra virgin olive oil, salt, pepper and the herbs. Cover with foil and place in the hot oven for 1 hour. Remove the foil and put back in the oven for about 20 minutes, until all the vegetables are cooked through.

Remove from the oven and serve with roasted meat.

# BREADS

For centuries, bread has been the staple of virtually every country and culture worldwide. The basic ingredients of flour, yeast and water and the ritual of kneading and proving the dough remains the same whether you make your dough by hand or use a machine.

My mother used to bake bread once a week in the big wood-fired oven; she would make enough to last the week. On bread-baking day, I would wake up to the wonderful aroma and rush downstairs to tear open a loaf of warm, freshly baked bread. Often she would make savoury breads, adding bits of leftover salami and cheese, similar to pane *contadino* (see page 158), or sometimes she would sweeten dough with some sugar and dried fruit as a treat for *merenda* (tea time).

In Italy every town and village has at least one *panetteria* (bakery) that bakes an array of breads and dough-based products each day – by lunchtime they have usually sold out. Years ago, if you did not have your own oven, boys would carry their family's precious cargo of bread dough to the *panetteria* on planks of wood covered in tea towels, to be placed in the hot oven and returned home as hot loaves.

Like most Italians, I enjoy bread with all my meals, from breakfast to supper, and could not imagine life without this most basic of foods. Italians consider bread to be almost sacred and never allow it to be thrown away; stale bread is always used up as bruschetta, fillings or made into breadcrumbs.

For me, making dough and baking bread is deeply satisfying. I love to wake up early and light the wood-fired oven in my garden. I then prepare the ingredients – I usually use fresh yeast, which I crumble into the flour, add water and watch the big bubbles explode as I mix it together. While the dough is rising I check the fire, add a few more logs if necessary, have my breakfast and get on with other things. This is the slowness when making bread. When the moment comes to shape the dough I like to be creative and use up leftovers such as grilled vegetables in *girelle* (see page 167) or use herbs from the garden in *panini al rosmarino* (see page 168). I love the smell of bread baking and it never fails to overwhelm me with sweet, nostalgic memories.

# Pane contadino
## Rustic farmers' bread

This is a country bread traditionally made by rural housewives for their husbands working in the fields. It was made using up leftovers of ham, salami, cheese and pork lard. In my region, we usually make this type of bread, with the addition of boiled eggs, at Easter; it is known as *casatiello* and is often made in large quantities to give away to friends and family. You can use any type of cured meats and hard cheese you have available – when I tested this recipe I didn't have any other Italian cheese, so I used up some Gruyère that I had in the fridge and the result was just as tasty.

Serves 6

500g/1lb 2oz/4 cups strong
  (bread) flour
1 x 7g sachet of dried yeast
3g salt
3g black pepper
2 tbsp extra virgin olive oil, plus extra
  to brush
300ml/10fl oz/1¼ cups lukewarm water
70g/2½oz pancetta, cut into small cubes
70g/2½oz coppa (or prosciutto), cut
  into small cubes
40g/1½oz salami, cut into small cubes
70g/2½oz Gruyère cheese, cut into
  small cubes
30g/1oz pecorino (romano)
  cheese, grated
30g/1oz Parmesan, grated

In a large bowl, combine the flour, yeast, salt, pepper and olive oil. Gradually add the water and mix well to form a dough. Knead on a lightly floured surface for 10 minutes, then leave to rest for about 5 minutes.

Meanwhile, mix together the cured meats and cheeses.

Open up the dough slightly, incorporate the cured meats and cheeses and knead for about 5 minutes, making sure all the ingredients are well combined. Form into a long sausage shape about 65cm/26 inches long and seal the ends together to form a ring. Place on a baking sheet, cover with a clean tea towel and leave to rise in a warm place for about 1 hour, until it has doubled in size.

Meanwhile, preheat the oven to 200°C/400°F/gas mark 6.

Brush the top of the bread with olive oil, reduce the oven temperature to 180°C/350°F/gas mark 4 and bake the bread for 35 minutes.

Remove from the oven and leave to rest for 10 minutes before serving.

Vg

# Focaccia di patate alla Pugliese
## Pugliese potato focaccia

Each Italian region has its own varieties of bread and focaccia. Puglia, the heel of Italy, is renowned for its amazing bread from the town of Altamura, but equally delicious is the potato-based focaccia. The addition of mashed potatoes makes the dough incredibly soft, and with its topping of cherry tomatoes this is a wonderful snack.

Makes 1 x 30cm/12-inch round focaccia

12g/¼oz fresh yeast
185ml/6½fl oz/generous ¾ cup
  lukewarm water
400g/14 oz/3¼ cups '00' flour
100g/3½oz potato, cooked and mashed
1 tsp salt

for the topping
100g/3½oz cherry tomatoes, halved
3 tbsp extra virgin olive oil
salt and freshly ground black pepper
1 tsp dried oregano
small handful of fresh basil leaves

Dissolve the yeast in a little of the water. Put the flour, mashed potato and salt in a large bowl, add the yeast-and-water mixture and gradually add the remaining water to form a smooth dough. Knead on a lightly floured surface for 5 minutes. Form into a ball, cover with clingfilm (plastic wrap) or a clean tea towel and leave to rise in a warm place for about 1½ hours, until it has doubled in size.

Meanwhile, preheat the oven to 200°C/400°F/gas mark 6.

Line a large baking sheet with greaseproof (waxed) paper or baking parchment, place the dough on top and, using your fingers, gently spread the dough to form a rough 30cm/12-inch circle; it will not be as thin as a pizza base. Top with the tomatoes, drizzle with olive oil, sprinkle with salt and pepper, oregano and the basil leaves. Bake for 30 minutes.

Remove from the oven and leave to rest for 5 minutes before serving. Enjoy hot or cold.

# Focaccia allo stracchino
## Cheese focaccia

This has to be one of the best focaccia around! It originates from Liguria and dates back to the Saracen raids in the ninth and tenth centuries, when locals fled the coastal areas to the safety of the mountains, where only basic ingredients such as flour, oil and cheese were available. Nowadays in Liguria this delicious cheese-filled focaccia is served warm as street food. Stracchino or crescenza, a soft cow's milk cheese, is used for this recipe. If you can't find it in your Italian deli, you can use Taleggio or, for a stronger flavour, dolcelatte. Make sure you stretch the dough as much as you can to get a really thin focaccia. Delicious served hot from the oven with a slice of mortadella.

Serves 4

500g/1lb 2oz/4 cups strong
  (bread) flour
1 x 7g sachet of dried yeast
6g sea salt
3 tbsp extra virgin olive oil, plus
  extra to grease and brush
250ml/9fl oz/1 cup lukewarm water
250g/9oz stracchino cheese,
  roughly chopped
salt and freshly ground black pepper

Mix the flour, yeast and salt in a large bowl. Make a well in the centre, add the olive oil and gradually add the water, mixing well with your hands to form a dough. Knead on a lightly floured surface for 15 minutes, until smooth and elastic. Cover with a clean tea towel and leave to rise in a warm place for 1 hour, until it has doubled in size.

Preheat the oven to 220°C/425°F/gas mark 7. Grease a 33 x 30cm/13 x 12-inch baking sheet with olive oil.

Divide the dough in two, making one piece a little bigger than the other. Take the larger piece and roll out into a roughly rectangular shape, then stretch by hand until it is about 3mm/⅛ inch thick. Line the greased baking sheet with the dough and pinch the edge to raise it to about 2cm/¾ inch high. Dot with pieces of cheese and sprinkle with a little salt and pepper.

Roll out the other piece of dough to the same thickness. Place over the cheese, pressing down with your fingertips and sealing the edges well. Brush olive oil all over the top and bake for 20 minutes, until golden.

Remove from the oven and leave to rest for a couple of minutes, then slice and serve.

Vg

# Focaccine con cipolle rosse

## Savoury buns with red onion

Although the Italian title suggests otherwise, these are not the thin bread we know as 'focaccia'– quite a few savoury breads in Italy are called focaccia. Very simple to make, the dough includes softened red onion, and is shaped into round buns and decorated with more red onion and a black olive. Delicious to eat by themselves or sliced and filled with mortadella or prosciutto to enjoy for lunch or a snack.

Makes 10 buns

4 tbsp extra virgin olive oil, plus
    extra to brush
1 large red onion, finely chopped, plus
    2 red onions, finely sliced, to garnish
700g/1lb 9oz/5½ cups strong
    (bread)flour
1 x 7g sachet of dried yeast
10g/¼oz/2 tsp salt
350ml/12fl oz/1½ cups lukewarm water
10 black olives, to garnish

Heat the olive oil in a pan, add the chopped onion and sweat for a few minutes until the onion has softened.

In a large bowl, combine the flour, yeast, salt and the softened onion. Gradually add the water and mix well to form a dough. Knead on a lightly floured surface for about 10 minutes. Form into a ball, cover with clingfilm (plastic wrap) and leave to rise in a warm place for 1 hour or until it has doubled in size.

Knead again for 5 minutes, then divide into 10 equal balls and gently press each with the palm of your hand to flatten slightly. Cover with a clean tea towel and leave to rise for 20 minutes.

Meanwhile, preheat the oven to 200°C/400°F/gas mark 6.

Decorate each bun with thin slices of red onion and a black olive, brush with olive oil and bake for 30 minutes, until golden brown. Leave to cool before serving.

# V

# Girelle con melanzane
## Aubergine bread rolls

These lovely rolls remind me of my early baking days when I would make bread rolls with whatever leftover vegetables I had around. The dough is rolled into a rectangular shape, topped with grilled aubergines (eggplants) and scamorza cheese, rolled up and cut into spiral rolls. It takes a little time to prepare but is really worth the effort. If you prefer, you can replace the aubergines with courgettes (zucchini) and the scamorza with mozzarella.

Makes about 15 rolls

12g/¼oz fresh yeast
1 tsp caster (superfine) sugar
3 tbsp lukewarm milk
300g/10½oz/ scant 2½ cups '00' flour
1 tsp salt
40g/1½oz/3 tbsp butter, melted
1 egg

### for the filling
500g/1lb 2oz aubergines (eggplants)
2 tbsp extra virgin olive oil, plus
    extra to grease
salt and freshly ground black pepper
150g/5½oz scamorza cheese,
    thinly sliced
a few basil leaves, torn

Dissolve the yeast and sugar in the milk and leave for about 10 minutes. Put the flour and salt in a large bowl, add the yeast mixture, melted butter and egg and knead on a lightly floured surface for about 10 minutes, until you have a smooth dough. Cover with a clean tea towel and leave to rise in a warm place for 1 hour or until it has doubled in size.

Meanwhile, prepare the filling. Preheat a grill (broiler) or griddle pan. Thinly slice the aubergine lengthways and grill on both sides. Combine the olive oil, salt and pepper and brush over the grilled aubergine. Set aside.

Lightly grease a large baking sheet and line with baking parchment.

Lightly flour a work surface and roll out the dough into a roughly rectangular shape. Top with the scamorza, aubergine and torn basil leaves. Carefully roll up lengthways, taking care that the filling does not escape, and leave to rest for 10 minutes. Using a sharp knife, cut into slices about 4cm/1½ inches thick, place on the prepared baking sheet, cover and leave to rest for 1 hour.

Meanwhile, preheat the oven to 200°C/400°F/gas mark 6. Bake the rolls for 15 minutes, until golden. Leave to cool before serving.

Vg

# Panini al rosmarino
## Rosemary bread rolls

Lovely bread rolls enhanced by the addition of rosemary make a welcome appearance in any bread basket. Delicious served with an antipasto of cured meats and preserved vegetables or simply as a snack on their own or with some creamy ricotta cheese. If you prefer, the rosemary can be replaced with black olives or, for a more pungent flavour, anchovy fillets – or a combination of all three – but if using anchovies you won't need to add the coarse sea salt.

Makes 12 rolls

500g/1lb 2oz/4 cups '00' flour
1 x 7g sachet of dried yeast
7g salt
3 tbsp extra virgin olive oil, plus
    extra to rub
250ml/9fl oz/1 cup lukewarm water
needles from 4 sprigs of rosemary
a handful of coarse sea salt

In a large bowl, combine the flour, yeast and salt. Add the olive oil and gradually mix in the water to form a dough. Knead on a lightly floured surface for 10 minutes, cover with a clean tea towel and leave to rise in a warm place for 1 hour or until it has doubled in size.

Using your hands, roll the dough into a long sausage shape about 2cm/¾ inch thick – it may be easier to divide the dough in two or three pieces before rolling. Rub a little olive oil all over, sprinkle with rosemary and sea salt, slice into sausage shapes about 20cm/8 inches long and wrap round into a coil. Press lightly with the palm of your hand and place the rolls on a baking sheet, cover with a clean tea towel and leave to rise for 1 hour.

Preheat the oven to 200°C/400°F/gas mark 6. Bake for 15–20 minutes, until golden. Cool on a wire rack.

# Pizza ai funghi e speck
## Wild mushroom and ham pizza

The secret to this pizza base is the sticky dough; it makes the resulting cooked pizza lovely and light. Don't worry about it being too sticky to handle, you don't have to knead it – if you prefer, wear some well-oiled latex gloves and you won't get the dough all over your hands. Make sure the top of the dough is well oiled before covering, otherwise the clingfilm (plastic wrap) will stick to it. Another tip when making this sticky dough is to use solid-based round or square baking sheets rather than the pizza trays with holes. In season, mixed wild mushrooms go really well with speck, a smoky cured ham from the Tyrolean region of northern Italy. If you can't find wild mushrooms, cultivated ones are delicious, too.

Makes 2 large pizzas

500g/1lb 2oz/4 cups strong
  (bread) flour
5g/1 tsp salt
10g/¼oz fresh yeast or 1 x 7g sachet
  of dried yeast
450ml/16fl oz/2 cups lukewarm water

**for the topping**
3 tbsp extra virgin olive oil, plus
  extra to grease and drizzle
1 garlic clove, finely chopped
½ red chilli, finely chopped
300g/10½oz mixed wild (or cultivated)
  mushrooms, cleaned and
  roughly chopped
salt and freshly ground black pepper
1 tbsp finely chopped fresh parsley
6 slices of speck (or other smoked ham),
  roughly torn
100g/3½oz Parmesan, grated

Put the flour and salt in a large bowl, crumble in the fresh yeast (or add dried) and gradually add the water to make a sticky dough. Cover the bowl with clingfilm (plastic wrap) and leave to rest in a warm place for about 30 minutes.

Generously grease two round baking sheets, about 33cm/13 inches in diameter, with olive oil.

Divide the dough in half and place each piece on a greased baking sheet, drizzle some olive oil over the dough, spread well, cover with clingfilm and leave to rest for at least 1 hour.

Meanwhile, make the topping. Heat the olive oil in a frying pan, add the garlic and chilli and sweat for a minute or so. Add the mushrooms, season with salt and pepper, and stir-fry for 4 minutes. Remove from the heat, stir in the parsley and set aside.

Preheat the oven to 230°C/450°F/gas mark 8.

Loosen the clingfilm over the pizza dough and use the clingfilm to spread the dough out on the baking sheet. Drizzle the dough with a little more olive oil, top with the mushrooms, ham and Parmesan. Bake the pizzas for about 7–8 minutes, slice and serve hot.

# V

# Pane dolce al cioccolato
## Chocolate brioche

A perfect treat for breakfast or *merenda* (tea time) for the children. The 'slowness' of this recipe is in the proving, which you must do twice for at least 2 hours; this will ensure the lightness of the brioche. The mixture is quite sticky to work with, so don't worry, this is how it should be and the results will be worth it. You can make the mixture by hand, but a mixer will be quicker. I prefer to use dark chocolate, giving the brioche a slightly bittersweet taste, but if you are making this for children, use a good-quality milk chocolate.

Serves 8

250g/9oz/2 cups strong (bread) flour
4g (½ sachet) dried yeast
50g/1¾oz/¼ cup caster
   (superfine) sugar
a pinch of salt
1 tsp ground cinnamon
4 eggs, beaten
200g/7oz/generous ¾ cup butter,
   softened and cut into small chunks
85g/3oz dark or milk chocolate,
   broken into 8 pieces
1 egg yolk
2 tbsp milk

Line a 20cm/8-inch diameter round cake tin with greaseproof (waxed) paper.

Put the flour, yeast, sugar, salt, cinnamon and 4 eggs in a mixer and whizz for 10 minutes. With the mixer still on, gradually add the butter and continue to whizz for another 5 minutes. Switch the machine off, transfer the mixture into a bowl, cover with clingfilm (plastic wrap) and leave to rest in a warm place for 2 hours.

The mixture will be quite sticky; however, form it into 8 equal balls. Insert a piece of chocolate into the centre of each ball, making sure the chocolate is completely covered with dough. Place the balls in the prepared cake tin, cover with clingfilm and leave to rest for 2 hours.

Preheat the oven to 180°C/350°F/gas mark 4. Combine the egg yolk and milk and brush over the top of the brioche. Bake for about 25 minutes, until golden brown. Leave to cool in the tin for 5 minutes, then turn out and break off the pieces.

# CAKES & DESSERTS

The traditional Italian meal nearly always ends with fruit; a bowl of fresh, seasonal fruits placed in the centre of the table for everyone to help themselves, so when I think of dessert, I naturally think of fruit. A lot of Italian sweet treats like *crostate* (tarts and pies) and cakes include fruit and for me there is nothing nicer than a home-baked dessert oozing with sweetness from ripe, seasonal fruit. Slowly cooked apples or pears undergo an amazing transformation from when they are fresh, and turning fruit into wonderful desserts has always been a pleasure for me.

My mother, sisters and grandmother loved to make sweet treats, especially on Sundays or feast days, and I was always sent to get the fruit because I knew where the best was to be found. I was the first to climb the fig trees and pick the ripest – I knew when this was because I used to check each day. The same went for cherries, plums, peaches, apricots, pears, apples – and during spring I would come home with basketfuls of wild strawberries, which grew on the hillside. I remember my mum used to fill jars with morello cherries, sprinkle them with sugar and leave them out in the sun for days until the sugar had dissolved; the result was a sweet cherry syrup which was used to fill pies or make cherry ices or simply serve as an accompaniment to cakes. This was effortless slow cooking, as the warm sunshine did the work.

My sisters often made *crostate*, which were slowly baked when the wood-burning oven was still warm from the day's bread baking. The smell of this home cooking was amazing, filling the house as well as our nostrils, and I couldn't wait for the delicacy to come out of the oven, constantly checking, so I could secure the first slice.

A lot of traditional desserts and cakes were made during festivities, in large quantities, to share with friends and family. For instance, at Easter the *pastiera di grano* (wheat and ricotta pie) was a favourite and women would spend entire days making them – and many still do. I like to maintain this tradition and I reserve a day before Easter Sunday to make a batch to give away and, of course, one or two to keep for my family.

A lot of Italian cakes and desserts, including *babà all'arancia* (see page 198) and the Italians' favourite Christmas cake, *panettone* (see pages 194-195), use yeast and require several slow risings; it is the slowness of the risings that give the desserts their lightness.

# V

# Meringa con zabaglione e fragole
## Meringue with zabaglione and strawberries

Meringue is so simple to make at home; with an electric whisk the mixture takes just minutes to prepare. The addition of a little lemon juice helps to keep the meringue shiny. You then pop it in the oven on a low temperature for several hours and go and do something else while the meringue slowly cooks. This is a large meringue nest; if you prefer to make smaller nests, cooking time would be reduced by about half. It makes a delicious dessert topped with Italian zabaglione and some fresh strawberries.

Serves 4

3 egg whites
a pinch of salt
200g/7oz/1 cup caster (superfine) sugar
½ tsp lemon juice
10g/¼oz/1½ tbsp icing (confectioners')
   sugar, sifted
200g/7oz strawberries, hulled
   and quartered

for the zabaglione
4 egg yolks
100g/3½oz/½ cup caster
   (superfine) sugar
3 tbsp vin santo or Marsala wine

Preheat the oven to 75°C/165°F/gas mark ¼ or as low as it will go. Line a 24cm/9½-inch diameter round baking sheet with baking parchment.

Put the egg whites and salt in a bowl and whisk until stiff peaks form. Gradually add the caster sugar, whisking all the time. Add the lemon juice and whisk until the sugar has dissolved. Put the mixture into a piping bag (pastry bag) and pipe a large nest onto the baking parchment. Alternatively, if you don't have a piping bag, you can use a large spoon. Sprinkle with icing sugar and immediately place in the oven for 4 hours.

Remove from the oven and leave to cool slightly before carefully removing from the baking sheet. Leave to cool.

Meanwhile, make the zabaglione. In a small heatproof bowl, whisk together the egg yolks, sugar and vin santo. Place over a saucepan of gently simmering water, whisking all the time until the mixture begins to boil and thicken. Remove from the heat, whisk well to get rid of any lumps, and leave to cool.

Put the meringue on a serving plate, fill the middle with the zabaglione and decorate with strawberries.

# V

# Crostata di albicocche e nocciole
## Apricot and hazelnut tart

If you like hazelnuts, you'll love this tart: ground hazelnuts are used in the pastry and the filling. It's simple to make but looks and tastes like a tart bought from a top pastry shop. Caramelizing the apricots gives extra flavour and colour. You can make the pastry a day or so in advance and store it in the fridge. The tart is delicious just as it is, or serve with mascarpone cream or good vanilla ice cream.

Serves 6

**for the pastry**

250g/9oz/2 cups plain (all-purpose) flour, sifted, plus extra to dust
a pinch of salt
125g/4½ oz/generous ½ cup cold butter cut into small pieces, plus extra to grease
100g/3½oz/½ cup caster (superfine) sugar
50g/1¾oz/⅔ cup ground hazelnuts
1 egg yolk

**for the filling**

450g/1lb apricots, halved or quartered
2 tbsp caster (superfine) sugar
100g/3½oz/7 tbsp butter, at room temperature
2 eggs
20g/¾oz/1½ tbsp plain (all-purpose) flour, sifted
100g/3½oz/1⅓ cups ground hazelnuts
100g/3½oz/¾ cup icing (confectioners')sugar

First make the pastry. Put the flour and salt in a large bowl and rub in the butter until the mixture resembles breadcrumbs. Mix in the sugar and hazelnuts. Add the egg yolk and 2 tablespoons cold water and work into a smooth dough. Form into a ball, wrap in clingfilm (plastic wrap) and leave to rest in the fridge for at least 20 minutes.

Preheat the grill (broiler). Put the apricots on a baking sheet, sprinkle with caster sugar and place under the hot grill for about 10 minutes, until caramelized. Set aside.

Preheat the oven to 170°C/325°F/gas mark 3. Grease a 24cm/9½-inch round tart tin and dust with flour.

To make the filling, put the butter in a bowl and beat until creamy. Whisk in the eggs one at a time, then whisk in the flour, hazelnuts and icing sugar until smooth and well combined.

Roll out the pastry on a lightly floured surface and line the prepared tin. Add the filling and top with the caramelized apricots. Bake for 45–50 minutes, until golden. Leave to rest for at least 10 minutes, then slice and serve.

# Torta gelata alle ciliege

## Cherry sponge dessert

This stunning dessert is halfway between a *semi-freddo* (ice cream) and a mousse and is perfect in spring/summer when cherries are plentiful. It's very simple to make and looks amazing. You make two plain sponge cakes and a cherry mousse-like filling, then assemble it – and the freezer does the rest. It can be made in advance and taken out of the freezer about 30–40 minutes before serving.

Serves 8

**for the sponge cakes**
3 eggs
150g/5½oz/¾ cup caster
   (superfine) sugar
1 vanilla pod, split lengthways
   and seeds scraped out
a pinch of salt
150g/5½oz/1¼ cups self-raising
   flour, sifted
butter, to grease
150ml/5fl oz/⅔ cup maraschino liqueur

**for the filling**
2 gelatine leaves
750g/1lb 10oz ripe sweet
   cherries, pitted
3 tbsp white wine
grated zest of ½ lemon
85g/3oz/scant ½ cup caster
   (superfine) sugar
300ml/10fl oz/1¼ cups double
   (heavy) cream, whipped

**for the topping**
7 tbsp apricot jam
150g/5½oz cherries, pitted and sliced
   in half
a few small mint leaves

Preheat the oven to 180°C/350°F/gas mark 4. Lightly grease 2 x 20cm/8-inch diameter round shallow cake tins and line with baking parchment. Line the bottom of a 20cm/8-inch diameter, 10cm/4-inch tall, loose-bottomed cake tin with baking parchment. Put the gelatine in a bowl of cold water to soften.

To make the sponge, whisk the eggs and sugar together in a bowl until light and fluffy. Fold in the vanilla seeds, salt and flour. Pour into the prepared shallow cake tins and bake for 15–20 minutes, until springy to the touch. Turn out and leave to cool on a wire rack.

To make the filling, put the cherries in a saucepan with the wine, lemon zest and sugar and cook on a medium heat, stirring all the time, until the cherries are very soft and the liquid has evaporated. Remove from the heat and blend until smooth. Squeeze the excess water out of the gelatine leaves and stir them into the cherry mixture until dissolved. Leave until cold, then add the whipped cream.

Put one sponge in the tall cake tin, smooth side down, drizzle over half the maraschino and pour in the cherry filling. Put the second sponge on top, smooth side up, gently pressing down with your fingers, and drizzle with the remaining maraschino. Cover with clingfilm (plastic wrap) and leave in the freezer for at least 2 hours.

Carefully remove the cake from the tin and place on a serving plate. Sieve the apricot jam and heat gently to make a smooth glaze. Brush the glaze over the top of the cake and decorate with cherries and a few mint leaves. Serve immediately or store in the fridge.

# V

# Cassata Siciliana al forno, di Elisabetta

Elisabetta's Sicilian baked cassata with ricotta
and chocolate

This recipe was given to me by my friend, Italian food blogger and exceptional pastry cook, Elisabetta Iudica. She just loves to bake and made this lovely Sicilian dessert for me. It is a lighter, less sweet variation of the traditional marzipan cassata; fresh ricotta and chocolate chips fill a delicate sweet pastry. Delicious as an after-dinner dessert or for afternoon tea, or, for me, with a freshly made espresso. Thank you, Elisabetta, for sharing your recipe and for keeping Italian cooking traditions alive and kicking in your food blog, La Mia Kitchenette.

Serves 8

**for the pastry**
300g/10½oz/scant 2½ cups '00' flour,
    sifted, plus extra to dust
½ tsp baking powder
a pinch of salt
150g/5½oz/generous ½ cup unsalted
    butter, cut into small cubes, plus
    extra to grease
150g/5½oz/¾ cup caster
    (superfine) sugar
1 egg
2 egg yolks
icing (confectioners') sugar, to dust

**for the filling**
500g/1lb 2oz/2 cups fresh ricotta,
    drained if necessary
200g/7oz/1 cup caster (superfine) sugar
30g/1oz dark chocolate chips

First make the pastry. Combine the flour, baking powder and salt in a bowl and rub in the butter until the mixture resembles breadcrumbs. Stir in the sugar, add the egg and yolks and work into a smooth dough. Alternatively, put all the ingredients in a food processor and whizz until they come together. Form the dough into a ball, wrap in clingfilm (plastic wrap) and leave in the fridge for a couple of hours.

Meanwhile, to make the filling, combine the ricotta, sugar and chocolate chips, but do not overmix. Cover with clingfilm and leave in the fridge until ready to use.

Preheat the oven to 170°C/325°F/gas mark 3. Lightly grease and flour a 20cm/8-inch round loose-bottomed cake tin.

Take about two-thirds of the pastry, roll out on a lightly floured surface and line the bottom and sides of the prepared tin. Using a fork, prick all over the pastry to prevent bubbles. Fill with the ricotta mixture, smoothing it over. Roll out the remaining pastry and cover the ricotta mixture, flattening it with your hand; seal around the edge with a fork, ensuring there are no gaps; the cake must be flat without a raised border.

Bake for 50–60 minutes, until golden all over. Leave to cool before removing from the tin and then leave for at least 2 hours before serving. Dust with icing sugar and serve.

# V

# Tiramisu al passito e arancia
## Tiramisu with passito and orange

This popular dessert can be seen on menus of Italian restaurants all over the world. It is usually made with espresso coffee and sometimes double (heavy) cream is added, too. To make it less calorific I have simply used mascarpone, which in itself is rich, and to give it a bit of a twist I have used orange juice and a little *passito*, a Sicilian dessert wine, to soak the biscuits. If you don't have *passito* you can use another sweet wine, or if making this for children, omit the alcohol altogether. Make sure you use fresh orange juice, as the bought stuff can be sweet and sickly. Simple to prepare, with no cooking involved, it's not an 'instant' dessert because it is best made the day before and left to set in the fridge.

Serves 4

1 egg yolk
1 tbsp caster (superfine) sugar
½ vanilla pod, split lengthways and
   seeds scraped out
250g/9oz/generous 1 cup
   mascarpone cheese
175ml/6fl oz/¾ cup freshly squeezed
   orange juice
1 tbsp passito, or other sweet wine
12 savoiardi biscuits
cocoa powder, sifted, to dust
grated zest of ½ orange

Combine the egg yolk, sugar and vanilla seeds in a bowl and whisk until creamy. Add the mascarpone and continue to whisk until well mixed. Set aside.

Combine the orange juice and wine. Dip the biscuits quickly into this liquid, letting them absorb a little but not too much, otherwise they will fall apart. Line a large glass dish or four individual dishes with some of the biscuits, followed by a layer of the mascarpone mixture and, depending on the size of your dish, continue making layers like this, ending up with the mascarpone. Dust with cocoa powder and top with a little orange zest. Leave in the fridge for at least 6 hours or overnight.

# V

# Pampapato
## Spiced chocolate treat

This nutty and spicy dense chocolate sweet treat originates from the province of Ferrara in Emilia-Romagna. The name *pampapato* means 'bread of the pope' because it was traditionally made in monasteries and convents and is shaped like the cap worn by the pope. Very simple to make, it is slow-baked at a low temperature. It is best made a couple of days before consuming. It is quite rich, so cut into thin slices when serving. Actually, it makes a nice energy snack when you're on the go and in need of a boost.

Serves 6

200g/7oz/generous 1½ cups plain
  (all-purpose) flour
100g/3½oz/⅔ cup whole almonds
100g/3½oz/generous 1 cup unsweetened
  cocoa powder
70g/2½oz/⅓ cup caster
  (superfine) sugar
50g/1¾oz/2½ tbsp runny honey
1 tsp mixed spice
20g/¾oz/2 tbsp raisins
125ml/4fl oz/½ cup milk
a little extra virgin olive oil, to rub
100g/3½oz dark chocolate

Preheat the oven to 150°C/300°F/gas mark 2. Line a baking sheet with greaseproof (waxed) paper.

Combine the flour, almonds, cocoa, sugar, honey, spice and raisins in a bowl. Gradually stir in the milk and mix well with your hands. Form into a domed shape about 12cm/5 inches in diameter, place on the prepared baking sheet, coat your hands with a little extra virgin olive oil and massage all over the *pampapato*. Bake for 1½ hours.

Remove from the oven and leave to cool completely.

Melt the chocolate in a heatproof bowl over a saucepan of gently simmering water and pour over the *pampapato*, spreading with a palette knife. Leave until set, and store in an airtight container until required.

# V

# Pere al forno con amaretti e mandorle

## Baked pears with amaretti biscuits and almonds

Italians love pears and in the autumn they often slow-cook the fruit, either on the hob or in the oven. This recipe is very simple to prepare; as the pears bake, their juices mix with the wine, cloves and lemon to produce a really delicious 'sauce'. The addition of almonds and amaretti biscuits give a nice crunchy texture. Serve the pears just as they are or with mascarpone cream, whipped cream or good vanilla ice cream.

Serves 4

4 large pears, such as Williams
    or Conference
175ml/6fl oz/¾ cup white wine
2 cloves
50g/1¾oz/¼ cup caster
    (superfine) sugar
grated zest and juice of ½
    unwaxed lemon
30g/1oz/¼ cup flaked (slivered)
    almonds, crushed
30g/1oz amaretti biscuits, crushed
½ tsp ground cinnamon
2 tbsp Marsala wine
30g/1oz/2 tbsp butter, divided into
    eight pieces

Preheat the oven to 180°C/350°F/gas mark 4.

Slice the pears in half lengthways and remove the pips, scooping out a little of the flesh. Set aside.

Combine the wine, cloves, sugar, lemon zest and juice in an ovenproof dish. Add the pear halves, cover with foil and bake for 1 hour, until the pears are cooked through.

Meanwhile, combine the crushed almonds, amaretti and cinnamon.

Remove the pears from the oven. Add the Marsala to the liquid. Fill the pears with the almond mixture, top each with a piece of butter, cover with foil and return to the oven. After 20 minutes, remove the foil and return to the oven for 10 minutes.

Leave to cool slightly before serving. Serve with the juice drizzled over the top and some mascarpone cream or ice cream if desired.

# V

# Ciambella alle mandorle
## Almond tea cake

This is similar to a tea loaf but round and plaited (braided) in traditional Italian *ciambella* style. Italian housewives often made a cake just like this one to use leftover bread dough. Not very sweet but with the subtle taste of almonds, this is a perfect tea time treat or delicious for breakfast with a cappuccino.

Serves 6–8

1 x 7g sachet of dried yeast
200ml/7fl oz/scant 1 cup lukewarm milk
600g/1lb 5oz/5 cups strong (bread)
    flour, plus extra to dust
½ vanilla pod, split lengthways and
    seeds scraped out
100g/3½oz/½ cup caster
    (superfine) sugar
100g/3½oz/1 cup ground almonds
100g/3½oz/¾ cup sultanas
    (golden raisins)
125g/4½oz/generous ½ cup
    butter, melted
60g/2¼oz/½ cup flaked
    (slivered)almonds
a little icing (confectioners')
    sugar, sifted, to dust

Check the instructions on the packet of yeast; if necessary, dissolve the yeast in the milk.

In a large bowl, combine the flour, vanilla seeds, sugar, ground almonds and sultanas. Make a well in the centre and gradually add the yeast and milk followed by 100g/3½oz/7 tbsp of the butter, mixing with your hands to form a dough. Knead on a lightly floured surface for about 5 minutes, cover with a clean tea towel and leave to rise in a warm place for 2 hours.

Divide the dough into three equal parts and roll each into a long sausage shape, roughly 55cm/22 inches in length. Plait the dough and join at the end to make a round cake. Line a baking sheet with baking parchment, put the ciambella on top, cover with a clean tea towel and leave to rise for 30 minutes.

Preheat the oven to 200°C/400°F/gas mark 6.

Bake the ciambella for 35 minutes. Remove from the oven, brush the top with the remaining melted butter, sprinkle with flaked almonds and return to the oven for 10 minutes. Leave on a wire rack to cool slightly and dust with icing sugar before serving.

# V

# Pastiera di grano
## Springtime wheat and ricotta pie

It is believed that this dessert dates back to pagan times, when ancient Neapolitans in springtime offered all the fruits of their land to the mermaid Partenope: eggs for fertility, wheat from the land, ricotta from the shepherds, the aroma of orange flowers, vanilla to symbolize faraway countries and sugar in honour of the sweet mermaid. It is said the mermaid took all these ingredients, immersed herself in the sea of the Bay of Naples and gave back to the Neapolitans a dessert that symbolized fertility and rebirth. The recipe as we know it today was first made in Neapolitan convents; the nuns would make it for the local nobility. Today in the region of Campania, Easter would not be the same without this traditional dessert. It is found in pastry shops all over the region and also made at home, usually in large quantities, to be given away as gifts to family and friends. The pre-cooked wheat is sold in jars in good Italian delis. Alternatively, you can make it with pearl barley, cooked according to the instructions on the packet. The pies can be made a few days in advance and stored in the fridge until required.

Makes 2 x 18cm/7-inch round pies; about 8 servings

**for the pastry**

250g/9oz/2 cups plain (all-purpose) flour, plus extra to dust
100g/3½oz/7 tbsp cold butter, cut into small pieces
100g/3½oz/½ cup caster (superfine) sugar
grated zest of 1 orange
2 egg yolks
a little milk, to brush
a little icing (confectioners') sugar, to dust

First make the pastry. Sift the flour into a large bowl and rub in the butter until the mixture resembles breadcrumbs. Stir in the sugar and orange zest, add the egg yolks and mix to form a smooth dough. Form into a ball, wrap in clingfilm (plastic wrap) and leave in the fridge for at least 1 hour.

To make the filling, put the wheat, milk, butter and cinnamon in a small saucepan on a low heat and bring to the boil, stirring all the time, until the wheat has absorbed all the milk and the mixture is creamy. Leave to cool.

To make the crema pasticciera, put the milk in a small saucepan together with the vanilla pod and place on a medium–low heat until the milk reaches boiling point. Meanwhile, whisk the egg yolks and sugar together in a bowl until light and fluffy, add the cornflour and whisk until smooth. When the milk reaches boiling point, remove from the heat, discard the vanilla pod and gradually pour the milk into the egg mixture, whisking all the time to prevent lumps from forming. Once well combined, pour the mixture back into the saucepan on a medium heat and stir with a wooden spoon. As soon as it begins to boil, remove from the heat immediately and leave to cool.

## for the filling

350g/12oz pre-cooked wheat or
   cooked pearl barley
150ml/5fl oz/⅔ cup full-fat milk
20g/¾oz/1½ tbsp butter
a pinch of ground cinnamon
350g/12oz/1½ cups ricotta
½ vanilla pod, split lengthways and
   seeds scraped out
250g/9oz/1¼ cups caster
   (superfine) sugar
grated zest of 1 orange
1 tbsp orange-flower water
3 eggs
2 egg yolks

## for the crema pasticciera

200ml/7fl oz/scant 1 cup milk
¼ vanilla pod
2 egg yolks
85g/3oz/scant ½ cup caster
   (superfine) sugar
20g/¾oz/2½ tbsp cornflour (cornstarch)

Take the wheat mixture and whisk in the ricotta, vanilla seeds, sugar, orange zest and orange-flower water; gradually mix in the eggs and yolks. Add the crema pasticciera and combine well together. Set aside.

Preheat the oven to 180°C/350°F/gas mark 4.

Roll out the pastry on a lightly floured surface and line 2 x 18cm/7-inch diameter round loose-bottomed pie dishes or shallow cake tins, reserving the trimmings. Pour in the wheat and ricotta mixture. Roll out the pastry trimmings and cut out long strips about 2cm/¾ inch wide; arrange these criss-cross over the pies. Brush a little milk over the strips, then bake for 50 minutes, until golden brown.

Switch the oven off and leave the pies to set in the warm oven for about an hour. Remove and leave to cool completely. Sift over some icing sugar before serving.

# V

# Torrone
## Italian nougat

Torrone is a nougat traditionally enjoyed at Christmas time in Italy; probably the most famous Italian torrone comes from Cremona in northern Italy, where legend has it that it was first made for an important wedding in the fifteenth century. Although torrone is normally bought from shops, you can make it at home. This recipe is a labour of love. Be prepared to spend a couple of hours stirring – ideally get someone to help you. You can flavour the torrone any way you wish – add candied fruit, orange zest, vanilla, cinnamon or coat it with melted chocolate. Slice in chunks, wrap in pretty tissue paper and ribbon and you have a lovely present.

Makes 500g/1lb 2oz

30g/1oz/3 tbsp shelled pistachio nuts
200g/7oz/1⅓ cups whole almonds, skinned
100g/3½oz/¾ cup whole hazelnuts, skinned
a sheet of rice paper
a little walnut oil, to grease 150g/5½oz/ scant ½ cup runny honey
150g/5½oz/¾ cup caster (superfine) sugar
2 egg whites
grated zest of 1 lemon (reserve the lemon)

---

**Toasting nuts**

Preheat the oven to 180°C/350°F/gas mark 4. Put the nuts on a baking sheet and toast for about 15 minutes, until light golden brown and crunchy. If you haven't been able to find skinned nuts, toasting will make it easy to rub off the skins. Set aside to cool.

First toast all the nuts (see tip). You will need a small loaf tin, about 19 x 8cm/7½ x 3¼ inches. Cut a piece of rice paper the same size as the bottom of the tin and another piece slightly larger and set aside. Lightly grease the sides of the tin with walnut oil and turn upside down so the oil doesn't run on the bottom of the tin.

Put the honey in a heaproof bowl and cook over a saucepan of gently simmering water (or use a double-boiler), stirring all the time with a wooden spoon for 1½ hours.

About 20 minutes before the end of this time, put the sugar and 3 tablespoons water in a small saucepan on a low heat for 15–20 minutes, stirring until the sugar has dissolved and is syrupy. In a clean bowl, whisk the egg whites until stiff. Gradually fold the egg whites into the honey, still cooking over simmering water, and stir well for 5 minutes. Gradually stir in the syrup. Continue to stir for 30 minutes.

Stir the nuts and lemon zest into the honey mixture. Line the loaf tin with the smaller piece of rice paper and pour in the honey mixture, pressing well with a wet spatula, then press well again with half a lemon. Put the remaining piece of rice paper over the top, pressing well with your hands. Leave to rest for 2 hours in a cool place – but not in the fridge.

Tip the torrone out of the tin onto a board and slice with a sharp knife. If you want to give the torrone as a gift, wrap it in greaseproof (waxed) paper and store in an airtight container for up to 2 months.

# V

# Panettone
## Traditional Italian Christmas cake

If you have ever wondered how to make your own panettone, and you enjoy a challenge as well as have a day to spare, this recipe is for you. The dough needs to rest at the end of each stage: this is what gives panettone its characteristic lightness. And of course you can get on with other things during these times. Ideally you will have a loose-bottomed panettone tin, 18cm/ 7 inches in diameter and 10cm/4 inches high – you could also use a slightly shallower and wider loose-bottomed cake tin.

There are many legends about how this cake originated and it appears that in ancient times the Romans sweetened a dough-like cake with honey; it is also said that poor people added a little dried fruit and sugar to bread dough as a Christmas treat. However, panettone as we know it today was created in Milan by two pastry chefs, Motta and Alemagna, in the early twentieth century. Its popularity spread over the years and it is produced industrially by many large companies, making it affordable for all Italians and becoming Italy's leading Christmas cake. In recent years it has evolved with flavourings such as chocolate, liqueur cream and others, but I find the original one with dried fruit and candied peel the best. In Italy panettone is traditionally served with a glass of *spumante* (light sparkling wine) at the end of the Christmas meal, but it is equally delicious with dessert wine or simply a nice cup of espresso or even tea.

Makes a 1.2kg/2lb 10oz cake

125g/4½oz/¾ cup sultanas
(golden raisins)
1 tbsp rum
12g/¼oz fresh yeast
150g/5½oz/¾ cup caster (superfine)
sugar, plus 1 tsp
4 tbsp lukewarm milk
500g/1lb 2oz/4 cups '00' flour
4 eggs, plus 3 egg yolks
150g/5½oz/generous ½ cup butter,
softened at room temperature, plus
a knob for the top
3g salt
40g/1½oz candied peel
grated zest of 1 lemon
1 vanilla pod, split lengthways and
seeds scraped out

### Step 1
Soak the sultanas with the rum and a little lukewarm water and set aside.

Dissolve 10g of the yeast together with 1 tsp sugar in the milk. Put 100g/3½oz/generous ¾ cup flour in a bowl, pour in the yeast mixture and work into a smooth dough. Form into a ball, cover the bowl with clingfilm (plastic wrap) and leave to rest in a warm place for about 1 hour, until it has doubled in size.

### Step 2
Add 2 eggs to the bowl, crumble in the remaining yeast, add 175g/6oz/1½ cups flour and mix well. Add 60g/2¼oz sugar and 60g/2¼oz butter and use your hands to incorporate all the ingredients to form a sticky dough. Form into a ball, cover the bowl with clingfilm and leave to rest in a warm place for 2 hours, until it has doubled in size.

**Step 3**

Drain and squeeze the excess liquid out of the sultanas and set aside.

Add the remaining 2 eggs, 3 yolks and the remaining flour to the dough and work with your hands for 10 minutes – the dough will still be quite sticky. Mix in the remaining sugar and the salt. Mix in 50g/1¾oz butter until well amalgamated, then add the remaining butter. Add the candied peel, lemon zest, sultanas and vanilla seeds. Mix well, cover the bowl with clingfilm and leave in a warm place for at least 2 hours, until the mixture has doubled in size.

**Step 4**

Meanwhile, lightly grease a loose-bottomed panettone tin, 18cm/7 inches in diameter and 10cm/4 inches high (or other cake tin) and line with baking parchment.

Turn the dough mixture onto a lightly floured work surface and work for a minute, then place in the prepared tin, cover with clingfilm and leave to rest in a warm place for at least 2 hours, until it has doubled in size.

Preheat the oven to 200°C/400°F/gas mark 6.

Using a small sharp knife, make a cross on the top and place a knob of butter in the middle. Place on the bottom shelf of the oven and bake for 15 minutes. Reduce the oven to 190°C/375°F/gas mark 5 and continue to bake for 45 minutes. If you notice the top of the cake getting too dark too quickly, reduce the oven temperature to 180°C/350°F/gas mark 4.

Remove from the oven and leave to cool slightly in the tin. Remove from the tin and leave to cool on a wire rack.

# V

# Babà all'arancia
## Orange-infused baba

Babà is a classic Neapolitan dessert which is usually made with rum. In my region, where lemons are plentiful, the pastry shops often make it with limoncello. For this recipe, I decided to give oranges a go and it really works well. Please note, you need to make this at least one day before you intend to serve it as it needs to dry out overnight before being soaked in the syrup.

Serves 10–12

10 eggs
40g/1½oz/⅓ cup caster (superfine) sugar
200g/7oz/generous ¾ cup butter, softened, plus extra to grease
600g/1lb 5oz/scant 2 cups strong bread flour, plus extra for dusting
a pinch of salt
40g/1½oz fresh yeast, dissolved in 2 tbsp lukewarm water

**for the syrup**
2 large oranges
400g/14oz/2 cups granulated sugar
1.5 litres/2½ pints/6¼ cups water
100ml/3½fl oz/scant ½ cup orange liqueur, or more if you prefer a stronger taste

**for the custard cream**
500ml/17fl oz/generous 2 cups milk
40g/1½oz/¼ cup cornflour (cornstarch)
large strip of orange peel
(blood oranges work nicely, too)
4 egg yolks
140g/5oz/¾ cup caster sugar
1 tsp vanilla extract

Grease a 22cm/8½-inch fluted babà or savarin mould with butter and dust with flour. Preheat the oven to 140°C/275°F/gas mark 1.

In a large bowl or stand mixer, whisk together the eggs and sugar until light and foamy, then whisk in the butter. Gradually add 500g/1lb 2oz of the flour and the salt, then, using your hands or the flat beater attachment, beat well until creamy. Add in the yeast liquid, followed by the remaining flour, and beat for a couple of minutes. Cover with a clean tea towel and leave to rise in a warm place for 30 minutes, until the mixture has doubled in size.

Stir the mixture once before pouring into the mould and leaving to rise in a warm place for 20 minutes. Bake the babà for 50–60 minutes until well risen and golden. Leave to cool in the mould, then turn out onto a wire rack and leave to dry out overnight.

Now, make the syrup. Using a vegetable peeler, peel the zest off the oranges in strips, setting aside a few pieces and cutting them thinner. Put the sugar in a saucepan, then stir in the water and orange zest on a medium heat until the sugar has dissolved. Bring to the boil, then reduce the heat and simmer for 1 hour. Strain through a fine sieve, add the orange liqueur and leave to cool.

Put the syrup in a container large enough to hold the babà. Very carefully, place the babà inside and drizzle the syrup all over the cake, then leave to soak for about an hour. Meanwhile, make the custard. Mix a little of the milk with the cornflour and set aside. Gently heat the remaining milk with the orange peel. Add the cornflour mixture to a separate saucepan, along with the egg yolks and sugar, placing on a low heat and whisking in the milk. Keep whisking until you obtain a thick, smooth custard. Remove from the heat, cover and leave to cool.

Carefully remove the babà, using a fish slice, and place on a serving plate. Decorate with the custard and reserved orange zest.

# PRESERVES

Preserving fruit and veg at the end of summer was a normal part of life when I was growing up. It was a way of keeping the scents and flavours of produce long after it was in season and was also a good reason to get together with friends and family – we celebrated the end of a bountiful season and went to work to preserve as much as we possibly could to see us through the winter. Bell peppers, aubergines (eggplants), courgettes (zucchini) and green beans were all preserved and we knew we would have to wait until the next summer before these vegetables reappeared in our gardens and market stalls. But also, in preserving, the taste changed, resulting in wonderful ingredients for antipasti or fillings for panini.

Our beloved tomato was the highlight of those late summer days – family and friends would gather together to bottle, sun-dry and make *concentrato* (tomato purée/paste) in the last of the hot summer sun. My job, as a boy, was to collect as many beer bottles as I could, in which to store a year-long supply of our local San Marzano tomatoes, grown around the Vesuvio area. Whole days would be spent carefully preserving tomatoes, and not just in our family: everyone in the village did the same – we even exchanged them as gifts to see whose tomatoes were nicer.

I still like to preserve as much as I can, and whenever I go on a mushroom hunt and strike lucky with basketfuls, I make sure they never go wasted and preserve them in oil to enjoy later in the year, usually at Christmas time. And when my friend Paolo has a glut of vegetables grown in his allotment, he shares them with me so they can be preserved. This year was it was beetroot and green beans. Markets are a great way of buying quantities of produce at good value, so if I see peppers or aubergines sold in bulk, as long as they are fresh, I buy them with preserving in mind.

Fruit, too, gets bottled; I love summer walks in the forest and fields and am always on the lookout for tiny damson plums, wild cherries and berries. Not only to be made into delicious jam but also to preserve in alcohol to liven up desserts.

Making preserves and bottling fruits and vegetables is a wonderful stress buster for me – not only do I enjoy foraging outdoors, I also love the ritual of preparing what I have collected, organizing the jars and putting them into my store cupboard. When the jars eventually get opened, each one has a story to tell – it may be where I picked that particular fruit or what sort of day it had been – and the taste of summer suddenly brightens up the dull of winter.

# Vg

# Zucchini crudi sott'olio
## Preserved raw courgettes

Makes 1 x 500ml/18fl oz/2¼ cup jar

500g/1lb 2oz courgettes (zucchini),
   sliced into long, chunky matchsticks
2 garlic cloves, sliced
1 tsp dried oregano
1½ tsp salt
½ red chilli, finely sliced (optional)
about 300ml/10fl oz/1¼ cups white
   wine vinegar
sunflower oil, to cover

Sterilize a 500ml/18fl oz/2¼ cup jar (see below).

Put the courgette matchsticks in a bowl with the garlic, oregano, salt, chilli (if using) and vinegar, making sure the vinegar completely covers the courgettes. Cover with a lid or greaseproof (waxed) paper, put a weight on top and leave to marinate for about 2 hours.

Drain off the liquid, reserving the garlic and chilli, and gently squeeze out the excess liquid from the courgettes. Place the courgettes together with the garlic and chilli in the sterilized jar and pour in the oil, making sure you completely cover the courgettes with oil. Secure with a lid, label and store in a cool, dark, dry place for at least 2 weeks before using. Once opened, store in the fridge.

### Preserving basics

• Always use very fresh, good-quality vegetables and fruit.

• To sterilize jars, wash and thoroughly clean all the jars and lids you are going to use, then rinse the jars with a little white wine vinegar. Leave to drain, then dry well. Place the jars and lids in a large pan of boiling water and boil for a couple of minutes. Remove, drain and dry well.

• To pasteurize: once you have placed the preserves in jars, seal well, preferably using hermetically sealed lids. Wrap each jar in old kitchen cloths: this prevents it from breaking during boiling. Line a large pan with kitchen cloth. Place the wrapped jars in the pan and add enough cold water to cover them by 3cm/1 inch. Bring the water to the boil, then reduce the heat to medium and boil for the time stated in the recipe. Turn off the heat, but leave the jars in the water until it is cold. Remove the jars and unwrap, then dry with a clean tea towel, label and store in a cool, dark, dry cupboard.

• Before you store your preserves, remember to label them with their name and the date you made them.

Vg

# Pomodori esiccati a casa
## Home-dried tomatoes

In southern Italy, where the summers are hot, it is common to see trays and trays of tomatoes drying out on people's balconies and roof terraces. The taste is amazing, much nicer than industrially made sun-dried tomatoes, and I always try to bring some back with me. In England, where the summers are not so reliable, you can recreate this way of drying by using the oven on a very low heat. These are best made towards the end of August, when plum tomatoes are plentiful. It's worth making quite a lot seeing as the oven has to be on for such a long time. Very simple to prepare: you put them in the oven and forget about them – even if they go over the 6 hours' cooking time, no harm will come to them. Smaller tomatoes will probably need less time. Once dried out, you can use them immediately or preserve them in oil.

2kg/4lb 8oz ripe but firm
   plum tomatoes
salt

Preheat the oven to 100°C/210°F/gas mark ¼ or lower. Line a baking sheet with greaseproof (waxed) paper.

Slice the tomatoes in half lengthways, place on the baking sheet, skin side down, sprinkle with salt and place in the oven for about 6 hours. If after this time there is still liquid left, leave in the oven for a little longer to dry out completely; this will depend on the size of the tomatoes.

Remove from the oven and leave to cool.

### Tips for using dried tomatoes

• Dress with extra virgin olive oil, garlic, fresh basil and dried oregano; add to a salad, top a bruschetta or pizza, or use in a pasta sauce.

• Preserve in sterilized jars (see page 202); make layers of dried tomatoes, basil leaves, a pinch of dried oregano and extra virgin olive oil, making sure you cover the tomatoes completely with the oil. Cover with a sterilized lid and store in a cool, dark, dry place.

# Vg

# Porcini sott'olio
## Preserved porcini mushrooms

Porcino, cep or penny bun – the king of the forest during the autumn mushroom season. The succulent, delicate taste of this highly prized fungi is hard to beat and always a winner with hunters and restaurateurs. I love to search for them in the forests and when I spot the first one, I'm like a child, excited and eager to find more. If I find lots, I usually enjoy a plateful sautéed or with some pasta, but the rest I preserve so that I can enjoy them later in the year and give them away as presents to friends. Preserved porcini are delicious served as part of an antipasto of cured meats, alongside other preserved vegetables.

Makes 1kg/2lb 4oz

1kg/2lb 4oz fresh porcini mushrooms
300ml/10fl oz/1¼ cups white
   wine vinegar
2 tsp salt
8 black peppercorns
4 bay leaves
1 sprig of thyme
2 cloves
1–3 red chillies (optional)
about 500ml/18fl oz/2¼ cups
   olive oil

Carefully clean the porcini, removing any earth and impurities with a small knife or brush, then go over them with a slightly damp cloth – don't wash the mushrooms or they will lose their lovely flavour. Trim the stems slightly; leave the smaller mushrooms whole and slice the larger ones.

Put the vinegar and 700ml/1¼ pints/2¾ cups water in a large pan together with the salt, peppercorns and bay leaves and bring to the boil. Add the porcini and boil for 4 minutes. Remove with a slotted spoon and leave to drain on a clean tea towel, cover with another clean tea towel and leave to dry out overnight.

Sterilize jars with a total volume of 1 litre/1¾ pints/ 4 cups (see page 202).

Put the mushrooms into the sterilized jars together with the thyme, cloves and a chilli (if using) and cover completely with olive oil. Secure with a lid and pasteurize for 30 minutes (see page 202). Label and store in a cool, dark, dry place for at least 1 month before using. Once opened, store in the fridge.

Vg

# Barbabietole sott'aceto

## Preserved beetroot in vinegar

Makes 1 x 1 litre/1¾ pint/4 cup jar

700g/1lb 9oz organic beetroot (beets)
a pinch of salt
450ml/16fl oz/2 cups white wine vinegar
½ celery stalk, finely sliced
15 juniper berries
5 black peppercorns
2 bay leaves

Sterilize a 1 litre/1¾ pint/4 cup jar (see page 202).

Wash the beetroot to remove all the dirt, place in a pan, cover with cold water, add some salt, bring to the boil and cook for 1½ hours, or until tender.

Drain and leave to cool. Carefully remove the skins, then slice the beetroot in halves or quarters and place them in the sterilized jar.

Put the vinegar and 3 tablespoons water in a small pan together with the celery, juniper berries, peppercorns and bay leaves. Bring to the boil, then boil for 3 minutes. Leave to cool, then pour over the beetroot in the jar. Secure with a lid and pasteurize for 20 minutes (see page 202). Label and store in a cool, dark, dry place for 2 weeks before using.

Vg

# Peperonata sott'olio
## Preserved peperonata

These tasty preserved peppers and tomatoes (photograph on page 204) are wonderful as part of a selection of mixed antipasto.

Makes 2 x 750ml/1¼ pint/3 cup jars

6 tbsp extra virgin olive oil
2 red onions, finely sliced
2 large garlic cloves, quartered
1 red chilli, finely sliced
1kg/2lb 4oz mixed (bell) peppers,
   sliced into thick strips
600g/1lb 5oz tomatoes, sliced
a handful of basil leaves
a pinch of salt
3 tsp capers
10 green olives
a pinch of dried oregano
about 400ml/14fl oz/1⅔ cups
   sunflower oil

Sterilize 2 x 750ml/1¼ pint/3 cup jars (see page 202).

Heat the olive oil in a saucepan, add the onions, garlic and chilli and sweat for a couple of minutes. Add the peppers, tomatoes, basil and salt, and gently stir. Cook on a medium heat for 5 minutes, then leave to cool.

Stir in the capers, olives and oregano. Fill the sterilized jars with the mixture and pour in enough sunflower oil to cover. Secure with lids and pasteurize for 25 minutes (see page 202). Label and store in a cool, dark, dry place. Once opened, store in the fridge.

# Vg

# Fagiolini della Regina Margherita
## Preserved green beans

Makes 1 x 600ml/20fl oz/2½ cup jar

400g/14oz green beans, topped
 and tailed
salt
375ml/13fl oz/generous 1½ cups
 white wine vinegar
1 clove
2 basil leaves
small strip of lemon zest
6 tarragon leaves
1 small shallot, cut in half
6 black peppercorns
1 garlic clove, left whole
1 red chilli (optional)
about 4 tbsp sunflower oil

Sterilize a 600ml/20fl oz/2½ cup jar (see page 202).

Bring a pan of lightly salted water to the boil, add the beans and boil for 3 minutes. Drain and leave to cool.

Put the vinegar, clove, basil, lemon zest, tarragon, shallot, peppercorns and garlic in a small pan. Bring to the boil, then boil for 1 minute. Remove from the heat and leave to cool.

Fill the sterilized jar with the beans, pour over the vinegar mixture and top with a little oil. Secure with a lid and pasteurize for 20 minutes (see page 202). Label and store in a cool, dark, dry place.

# Vg

# Marmellata di limone
## Lemon marmalade

I grew up with lemons – the best type, too, from Amalfi. We used them in a lot of our cooking, for medicinal purposes or just sliced and eaten on their own. Strangely, though, lemon marmalade was not made; it was not until I came to England that I discovered the delights of marmalade. In more recent years, oranges and lemons, which grow in abundance in southern Italy, have begun to appear in the form of jams and preserves. This lemon marmalade is really simple to make; the secret is to buy the best lemons you can find. It is not only good on toast, but is also delicious served with cheese. This recipe is very natural and a must for lemon lovers – if you prefer a less bitter taste, I suggest you boil the lemon peel another couple of times in addition to the one mentioned in this recipe.

Makes about 500ml/18fl oz/2 cups

1kg/2lb 4oz unwaxed organic lemons
500g/1lb 2oz/2½ cups granulated sugar

Wash and dry the lemons well, then peel and set the peel aside. Remove and discard the pith. Slice the lemons very finely, discarding any pips. Place in a non-metallic container. Add the sugar and mix well together, cover with clingfilm (plastic wrap) and leave to macerate for 12 hours.

Sterilize jars with a total volume of 500ml/18fl oz/2 cups (see page 202).

Finely chop the peel and place in a pan with water to cover, bring to the boil, then boil for 1 minute. Drain well.

Put the peel and sugary lemons in a saucepan and cook on a low heat for about 1 hour, until the marmalade begins to thicken. Remove from the heat, pour into sterilized jars, cover with lids, turn upside down and leave until cold. Label and store in your cupboard. Once opened, store in the fridge.

**Vg**

# Lamponi e mirtilli sotto spirito
## Raspberries and blueberries preserved in alcohol

I love to preserve summer fruit and enjoy it during the winter, when these fruits and the long sunny days are a distant memory. Soft fruit preserved in alcohol makes an extra special treat, especially at Christmas time, to serve as a dessert with some mascarpone or double (heavy) cream or as an accompaniment to chocolate cake or citrus tart. You can use the same method for cherries and tiny plums. You can also drink the fruit-infused alcohol, but please, be careful, not too much! You can buy pure alcohol from good Italian delis.

Makes 3 litres/12½ cups/3 quarts

500g/1lb 2oz raspberries
500g/1lb 2oz blueberries
1 litre/1¾ pints/4 cups pure alcohol
800g/1lb 12oz/4 cups granulated sugar
zest of 1 orange, peeled in long strips
zest of 1 lemon, peeled in long strips

Put the berries in a large bowl, add the alcohol, cover with clingfilm (plastic wrap) and leave in a dry, dark place for 3 days.

Sterilize 3 x 1-litre/1¾-pint/4-cup jars (see page 202).

Put 1 litre/1¾ pints/4 cups water in a saucepan with the sugar, orange and lemon zests and place on a gentle heat, stirring until the sugar has dissolved. Leave to cool completely and then strain through a fine sieve.

Drain the fruit, reserving the alcohol. Combine the alcohol with the strained sugar syrup. Put the fruit in the sterilized jars to about one-third full, then add the liquid until the fruit is covered. Cover the jars with their lids and label. Leave for at least a month before using. Before serving, place in the fridge to enjoy cold.

# Index

# Dedication

To Jamie Oliver, who once learned from me and now I learn from him.

# Acknowledgements

Thanks to: Liz Przybylski, for writing; Adriana Contaldo, for testing recipes; Laura Edwards for the photography; Pip Spence for cooking and styling at the photoshoot; Laura Russell, Ellen Simmons, Kom Patel and the team at Pavilion Books; Luigi Bonomi; Enzo Zaccarini at Vincenzo for their lovely fruit & veg.

———

Pavilion
An imprint of HarperCollins*Publishers* Ltd
1 London Bridge Street
London SE1 9GF

www.harpercollins.co.uk

HarperCollins*Publishers*
Macken House
39/40 Mayor Street Upper
Dublin 1, D01 C9W8
Ireland

10 9 8 7 6 5 4 3 2 1

First published in Great Britain by Pavilion
An imprint of HarperCollins*Publishers* 2024

ISBN 978-0-00-869561-3

Publishing Director: Laura Russell
Commissioning Editor: Ellen Simmons
Editorial Assistant: Shamar Gunning
Proofreader: Anne Sheasby
Photography: Laura Edwards
Food and Prop Stylist: Pip Spence
Junior Designer: Lily Wilson
Production Controller: Grace O'Byrne

Printed and bound in China